KEN DRUSE THE PASSION FOR GARDENING

KEN DRUSE THE PASS

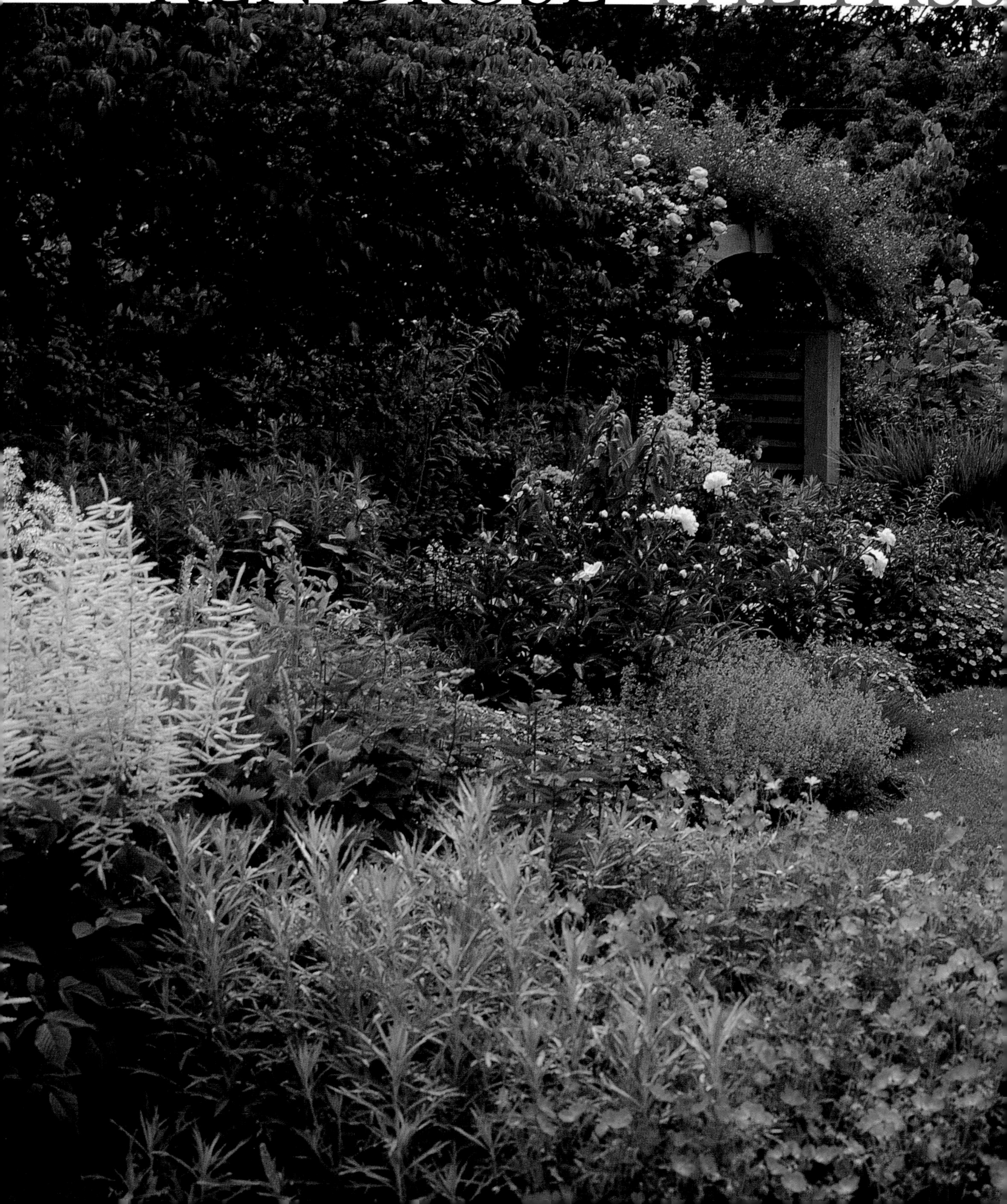

ION FOR GARDENING

INSPIRATION FOR A LIFETIME

KEN DRUSE
WITH
ADAM LEVINE

Clarkson Potter/Publishers
NEW YORK

Published by Clarkson Potter/Publishers, New York, New York
Member of the Crown Publishing Group, a division of Random House, Inc.
www.randomhouse.com

CLARKSON N. POTTER is a trademark and POTTER and colophon are registered trademarks of Random House, Inc.

Printed in China

Design by Jane Treuhaft

Library of Congress Cataloging-in-Publication Data
Druse, Kenneth.
    Ken Druse: the passion for gardening / Ken Druse with Adam Levine.—1st ed.
Includes bibliographical references
1. Gardening.   2. Gardens.   I. Levine, Adam.   II. Title.
    SB455 .D78   2003
635—dc21   20020141 44

ISBN 0-517-70788-8

10   9   8   7   6   5   4   3   2   1

First Edition

The vivid leaves of red castor bean, *Ricinus communis* 'Red Spire', OPENING PAGE, against the red garage wall in John Beirne's garden (pages 179–87). PRECEDING PAGES: Phyllis and Howard Kramer's incredible perennial border in Rhode Island. OPPOSITE: Plants arrive via mail from Gossler Farm and Nursery in Eugene, Oregon, at my garden in New Jersey. FOLLOWING PAGES, LEFT: A little fern finds a tiny niche on the edge of a garden pool. RIGHT: I often say gardening is a matter of trowel and error. I need to feel the soil, so as soon as wooden handles are set down, the gloves come off.

ACKNOWLEDGMENTS

To produce this book, I sought gardeners who discovered one of several essential aspects to their passion. I felt there was a need to describe things that lead us beyond exterior decoration, to gardening as a way of life. Some of these aspects to our passion became the titles of chapters in this work. To my surprise, each of the people in this book had discovered all of these elements. I want to thank the wonderful people who shared their creations and lives with me. ❦ Writing this book was necessary, but most remarkable was that Clarkson Potter Publishers saw the importance of new kind of garden book—neither a passive tour guide nor an aggressive how-to tome. My thanks go to Jenny Frost, Lauren Shakely, Marysarah Quinn, Amy Boorstein, Mark McCauslin, Robin Slutzky, Joan Denman, Merri Ann Morrell, Lance Troxel, Jennifer DeFilippi, and Leigh Ann Ambrosi. ❦ The careful work of Jane Treuhaft, Clarkson Potter's Associate Art Director and the designer of this book, are evident on every page. Less apparent is the hard work and attention to detail of my editor, Roy Finamore, who made creating this book a smooth process. ❦ I am obliged to Fuji film and Duggal Color Labs (CH) for their technical contributions. I want to also extend my appreciation to George Waffle and Peter D'Aquino of my studio. Peter keeps track of our 150,000-photo library. George keeps track of everything else, including me when I am on the road. I would also like to thank Gretchen Grant, Scott Kolber, and Geoff Mayo for unfailing confidence, and Louis Bauer for again providing horticultural guidance and gardening wisdom. ❦ I am most grateful to my collaborator on the text, Adam Levine. We discussed every aspect of our devotion to gardening, and Adam introduced me to more people who are as obsessed as we are.

Now, I want to share the most important thing I learned with all readers: You don't need permission to make a work of art in your own backyards, and with hope, the process will never be finished.

CONTENTS

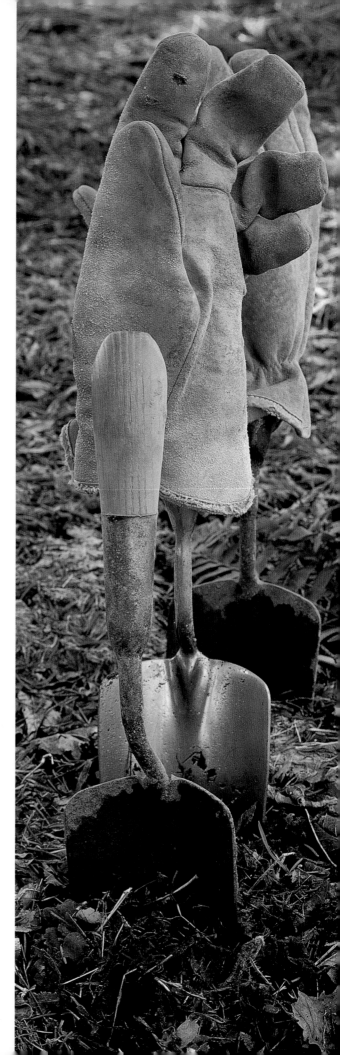

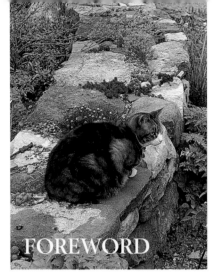

Gardening is my passion. If I could indulge myself in it for every waking hour for the rest of my life, it would not be enough time to learn all I want to know or grow all the plants I dream about. Sometimes I feel a little guilty when I spend time playing in the soil, rather than attending to all the myriad things screaming for my attention. For one thing, if I'm out in the garden, I'm not getting a paycheck. But when I have such doubts, I remind myself that this pursuit—at once art and science and, when practiced with care, conservation—is worthy of a lifetime of work. ❦ I feel this way for a

number of reasons, some of which form the basis of this book. Rather than a volume full of "how-to" information, *The Passion for Gardening* is a why-to book—why we garden, and the many ways our lives are enriched by choosing this path. In talking to the various gardeners profiled in these pages, what I had long suspected became crystal clear: there seems to be an underlying spirit of gardening that all of us share, regardless of the kind of garden we choose to make. You easily know the difference between day-to-day life, and really living: think about "having a garden" and gardening. Like the best parts of cooking, the process of making a garden is often more enriching than the product, and the results are arguably even more pleasing since they are never consumed, and may last your lifetime or longer. For many of us, this synergy between garden and gardener—the attitudes and methods with which we choose to practice horticulture and nurture living things—is the goal in itself.

The benefits of planting and tending plots of earth are abundant and available to everyone. Medical research shows that simply looking at a garden is good for your health: watching butterflies and seeing colorful flowers lower blood pressure. Fragrances stimulate us, as do colors; some are exciting, others calming. The psychological importance of connecting with nature, brought to us in gardens, also cannot be ignored. In the days following September 11, 2001, New York City's public gardens reported higher than usual attendance. In a time of destruction, people found comfort in reminders of nature's power to regenerate—in plants to grow.

Tending the soil with busy hands sets the mind free to dream and can soothe the spirit like no other pursuit. The siren call of our chaotic lives recedes into the background while we prune or harvest or simply putter among the plants. Gardening takes a certain amount of concentration, but between hand and eye there is a space for the mind to drift. Thoughts germinate, along with visions of gardens past and those to be. We mull over the events of the day, interpret things we heard or said, contemplate decisions great or small. Repetitive activities such as weeding might look tedious and unfulfilling to the uninitiated but they can attain a certain rhythm, become a form of moving meditation in which hours may go by without notice.

Candelabra primroses (*Primula* sp.), darmera with wide leaves, and variegated iris and sweet flag fill my canal garden in New Jersey, PRECEDING PAGES, LEFT. Peach the cat oversees the gravel garden, RIGHT. Visitors to Old Westbury Gardens on Long Island, ABOVE, take pictures, make notes, and meet gardeners to get ideas for their home plantings. OPPOSITE: Hothouse geraniums (*Pelargonium* sp.), tended by Adam Levine, fill an old greenhouse on an estate near Media, Pennsylvania.

You are never too young to garden, or too old. As a child you might have planted a seed in a paper cup, or grown an avocado from a pit, or sowed sunflower seeds outdoors and marveled at how they towered overhead by summer's

end. Later you might have planted bigger things, like trees, and watched them grow taller than you are, through adolescence and into maturity.

As we grow, the garden grows and changes with us. When we are young and strong, we build stone walls, we dig deep to turn compost into the soil. As we get older, parts of the garden may need to be reconfigured to make caring for the plants more comfortable. Steps can be converted into gentle slopes; and we can add raised beds for planting so that stooping and bending are all but eliminated. Tools and techniques are available to allow gardeners of all ages and abilities to continue tilling the soil.

The more we garden, the more we learn. We learn by visiting gardens and nurseries; from mail-order catalogs, picture books, encyclopedias, garden magazines, and other media. With eyes wide open, we learn from art, history, travel, science—from anything that excites our curiosity. Everything that happens in our gardens, no matter how brutal or benign, teaches some lesson or another, and our gardens are transformed by this knowledge.

Over time we discover which plants we like and which we don't, and find that certain garden styles complement our lives better than others. Gardening then becomes a matter of refinement, of winnowing through the choices to find those that mirror our true desires. The monotony of lawn maintenance might be traded for tending a collection of dwarf evergreens or producing a voluptuous perennial border. The diversion becomes a passion that is more fulfilling than nearly any other leisure-time activity.

Adam Levine, my co-writer on this book, is devoted to the genus *Pelargonium*. These plants are geraniums, not the herbaceous kinds of northern gardens but frost-tender evergreen shrubs. Unless a garden is in a climate they like, such as their homeland in South Africa or in San Francisco, they must be grown under glass in greenhouses, on cool windowsills, or under lights. His interest spread from this genus to all manner of tender perennials in containers, which spend summers outdoors on his patio and winters in an old greenhouse lent to him by his landlords. This partnership allows Adam the opportunity to grow his favorite plants, and his landlords to share in the enjoyment of the results.

The gardening world is full of such collaborations. Gardeners like to trade information and advice, to give away pieces of their favorite plants and acquire new favorites from friends. But foremost is the collaboration that all gardeners have with nature. A gardener's expression comes from laying hands on the natural world. We paint in the colors of plants, sculpt in soil, rock, water, and air. Nature is our muse and partner, but we all learn soon enough that our role is to be the junior partners in this relationship. As gardeners, we have an opportunity to improve more than the aesthetics of our environment. I see it as our responsibility to garden in a new way: one that nourishes the Earth at every step, rather than depleting it. Topsoil can be enriched with homemade compost. Local plants can be aided in their attempts to reclaim homes lost through development. We can plant for other animals and insects. By following a horticultural version of the Golden Rule, always striving to leave things better off than we found them, we can contribute to the welfare of future generations. We not only have to try to bend other adults to these new ways, but need to teach them to the next generation. Sharing our passion for gardening and nature with children is like planting seeds of hope for the future.

Even while gardening with consideration for nature, the opportunities for creativity are still boundless. You can dream big in a garden, experiment, make mistakes, and find success for yourself and others. Gardening presents opportunities for self-expression and the pleasure that comes from creating a thing of beauty. Aesthetic risks are rarely permanent but often thrilling. You don't have to take that less-than perfect creation—for instance, a rudimentary trellis constructed early in your career—and store it in the attic. Plant a rose to cover the first attempt while you build a better one for another spot. A plant that blooms slightly off color from your envisioned scheme can be moved to a spot that suits it and another one brought in to complete your composition.

I know at once if I like a garden, and my reaction has nothing to do with whether there are meticulously maintained beds and borders or a flock of pink flamingos guarding the gate.

It isn't the style, the plants used, the location, or the size. What matters to me is the passion of the garden's tender, which comes through loud and clear over anything else. Such gardeners love plants not just for their color or form, but because they are alive. These gardeners are not afraid of change; on the contrary, it is a crucial part of their fascination with gardening. More than simply tilling the soil, these people are the guiding spirits whose devotion makes a garden more than a backyard, or the back forty.

Our artistic endeavors are subject to nature's whim, even to disaster and destruction. I try not to underestimate nature's energy: it is the power of the garden and the center of us all. As a living work of art, a garden is never static. But I am not disappointed by the idea that my creation is, in some ways, like a sand castle on the beach. My garden is always moving and changing, in tune with the world around it, and I get to both witness this endless mutability and grow along with it. This process, this evolution, not only reminds me that I am alive. It is life.

PART 1

RECREATION FOR A LIFETIME

I met a young horticulturist at a botanical garden recently, and we spent several minutes chatting about the plants she helped to tend. We were meeting on common ground—as two garden lovers—and we both chattered on excitedly, sharing ideas about culture and information about little-known species that we'd both learned to love. But when she mentioned that she grew one of these species on the windowsill of her parents' house, where she lives, and that she hoped someday to have a garden of her own, I suddenly felt every one of my fifty-plus years. I wondered how she viewed me, dreading the idea that she saw me as a contemporary of her father (which I was). I wanted to seem cool, but then I had an awful thought: Good God, I've got houseplants older than this girl!

I mentioned this encounter to my friend Jill Hagler, who is halfway in age between me and the young gardener. "It's just a state of mind," she assured me. "All gardeners are young at heart." And it's true: all the gardeners I know always seem to have one foot in the future, wondering what gifts they'll get from the garden tomorrow, next week, and next year. Gardening truly is a lifetime recreation, one that can keep us fresh and on our toes (or on our knees) until the end of our days.

Among my older-than-the-young-gardener houseplants are twin specimens of the cycad *Zamia furfuracea*, which were probably five or ten years old when I bought them in 1975. They traveled with me from my first college apartment in Providence, Rhode Island, to Manhattan and then to Brooklyn. Now the twins live in New Jersey, and their longevity helps put our history of gardening together into perspective. Ancestors of these conifers populated the earth for millions of years before flowering plants evolved. The fact that this genus has been around for so long points out how very short thirty, forty, or fifty years is, and how my time on earth spent in the garden is really only an instant in the scheme of things.

I may call thirty years an instant, but in this age—which might be called the "Age of Impatience"—that span of time may as well be forever to most people. We get impatient if the car in front of us pauses imperceptibly at a red light. We watch the interminable seconds

tick away on the microwave, and get irritated if the computer takes a few extra nanoseconds to accomplish a task that, even five years ago, would have seemed incomprehensible. Technology has compressed time so greatly that we have come to expect miracles to be over and done with almost before we even notice they have begun.

Gardening is an antidote to this manic pace. Gardens aren't created overnight; a good garden takes time to develop, and then can be made and remade, over the course of a lifetime and even into succeeding generations. Plants don't mature in nanoseconds. They follow the pace of the natural world, which for most of time has been the only measure of time: the passage of days and seasons, the annual cycle of death and rebirth. The late May Sarton, whose intimate journals are full of wisdom about life in the garden, wrote: "Everything that slows us down and forces patience, everything that sets us back into the slow cycles of nature, is a help. Gardening is an instrument of grace." Tending a garden can be a continual lesson in letting go, of accepting what is offered and appreciating the moment—because a moment later, what you see could disappear. How many times has some wonderful thing become a casualty of a thunderstorm or been decapitated in an unfortunate dog-walking incident? The list of possible accidents is endless, and even the plants themselves have a built-in brevity: *Hemerocallis* aren't called daylilies for nothing.

Unfortunately, many promoters of garden products hope to cash in on our cultural impatience, offering "new" ideas for instant color, instant effect, instant solutions. For many people, quick-kill herbicides in disposable spray bottles have replaced hand-weeding tools; the annoying whine of the electric- or gas-powered blower has largely obliterated the gentle "scccrick" of the rake. Gardening magazines try to be about "The Garden" without getting into the dirty business of "gardening," featuring articles with seductively impossible titles such as "101 Easy Ideas for a No-Maintenance Landscape." One Internet purveyor (now out of business) perhaps epitomized this attitude, offering pre-chilled daffodil and tulip bulbs to plant in the spring for "instant" bloom. The company claimed that this would allay the "sense of failure" gardeners feel when they plant bulbs in the autumn and have to wait months to see the rewards of their efforts.

This attitude devalues the appeal that gardening holds for many of us. It assumes that making a garden is as simple as putting up Christmas decorations: buy a few gewgaws, plug them in, turn them on, and then move on to the next activity. It promotes decorator gardens full of "colorful plant material," which are "installed" (as if they were appliances) to one-up the Joneses and then ignored until they need to be freshened up and dusted off for the next party. Yes, there will always be fashions, fads, and trends in gardening. We only need to look at a Victorian-era seed catalog to see all the plants that have come and gone and come back into favor again. But gardening itself will never be a fad, as the long-term involvement of so many of us makes amply clear.

While a beginning gardener might fall for these advertising gambits, anyone who has gardened for even a little while knows that good things don't come easily, and rarely in an instant.

Raised beds may be just the help older gardeners need, ABOVE, bringing the earth a little closer to aging hands, backs, and knees. OPPOSITE: My old Brooklyn backyard garden as it appears from a second-story window.

What so many jaded marketers fail to imagine is the rich relationship between the gardener and the garden, how dedicated we can be to our favorite pastime. They don't see that many of us actually like getting our hands in the dirt. They don't understand that looking ahead, anticipating future rewards that will sprout from our efforts of the moment, is part of the wonderment of gardening for us. We don't want to get out of the garden in less time. Most of us want *more* time to spend puttering in our beds. I'd like to ask those garden-product executives: Would you have bothered to learn how to play tennis, or golf, so you could play just one game and then retire your rackets and clubs to the attic?

Have you ever seen a garden trowel used only once?

GARDEN OF THE MIND

It is ironic that when the garden we dreamed of creating finally seems finished, the picture keeps changing. Other artists don't have this problem. A painting, a sculpture—these are worked until the creator decides the piece is finished, at which point it doesn't continue to mutate into something else. Displayed in a climate-controlled museum, such a work of art will remain basically unchanged for hundreds of years. But gardeners can't control the climate. On the contrary, it controls us, determining what we can do and how long we can stand to be out there doing it. A garden can't be protected from the elements, since those elements are what it needs to survive. A garden is alive, with plants in different stages of life. Some are growing old and senescent, some reaching a distinguished maturity, and some merely babes in the woods, just starting to spread their branches and roots.

Because of this endless mutability, gardening—more than any other art—is as much about the process as the end result. It can be disconcerting to visit a garden deemed "historically significant" and fixed in that arbitrary time, as if gardeners of historic importance would not have continued to evolve—ripping up their beds and replanting them based on new knowledge, new plants, even new fashions. How a famous architect chose to arrange a living room might be insightful, but outdoors, the garden is a "living" room that never has a set moment in time.

"In a garden, you learn that nothing is static," says Juana Flagg, who has gardened on the same Connecticut property for nearly half a century. "There's no such thing as instant landscaping. It's always changing, never ending."

When I began the Brooklyn garden described in my book *The Natural Shade Garden*, I thought I would design it, plant it, and enjoy it. I moved in too late in the fall to do anything outside, so I had all winter to plan and sketch and dream—and I dreamed big. I wanted a folly—a combination classical ruin and summer house. I needed a barbecue area, a dog run, a pond with a bridge. I wanted thousands of different plants—trees and shrubs, vines and groundcovers, annuals, perennials. I wanted it all—all in a backyard measuring 21 by 50 feet.

These twin *Zamia* plants have accompanied me from garden to garden for nearly thirty years, OPPOSITE. Relatives of these slow-growing prehistoric plants survived the extinction of the dinosaurs, and these two have thrived in my gardens in Rhode Island, New York City, and Brooklyn, and now live in the mountains of northwestern New Jersey.

Eventually it didn't matter what I got or didn't get, because after ten years, I was still doing it—trying different plants, digging a larger pond, pruning, moving things around. The only thing that

slowed down my delighted tinkering was starting another garden somewhere else, after which the one in Brooklyn became a somewhat neglected adolescent. But it was also the babysitter and parent of a number of plants for the new garden in New Jersey, some of which had earlier been part of my rooftop garden in Manhattan. Think of those *Zamias*, tagging along with me through four gardens.

Some people grow attached to a piece of land and could never dream of moving elsewhere. It is unlikely that landscape designer Tom Rooks will move from his acres in Michigan, or that Juana Flagg, nearing eighty, will be looking to start a new garden elsewhere. (Both these gardeners are profiled in this section.) But other gardeners would happily move to a site that appealed to them more than the one they now tend. The longing is often for a garden that has whatever the present one lacks: more sun or more shade; more space, or, as we grow older, perhaps less space; a patch of woods, a meadow, a pond, a stream. Many of us have our "dream gardens," but if that dream ever materializes, the reality of it may not equal our fantasies, and we might begin to long for something else.

A friend once asked if I thought I would grow old in my New Jersey garden, and was surprised when I said that I didn't know. I love this place—the river, the island, my neighbors—

but I am already dreaming of the next place. I've moved several times in my life, and I don't miss any of my former "gardens"—my menagerie of houseplants in Rhode Island and their summering place in the light well of a tenement building; the 80-by-100 foot rooftop in Manhattan's SoHo neighborhood; the Brooklyn backyard.

One reason I don't miss these gardens is because I've learned, through the years, that my plants can come with me. That many plants, or pieces of them, can be uprooted and moved, either across the yard or across the country, is something that few beginners are taught, and few things in gardening terrify them more. As with pruning (which many beginners see as an act akin to mutilation), confidence in digging and moving plants comes with experience. As we have our first tentative success, and see the plant (which we once held in our

For many people, spring means the pink, orange, and magenta of Asian azaleas. But spring colors in Judy Glattstein's woodland garden, RIGHT, are arguably more subtle: the chartreuse of leaves emerging from the ground, and the shades of ephemeral wildflowers such as her beloved trillium. When her husband's new job meant relocating, Judy dug up and potted as many plants as possible to bring to the next safe haven.

hands, exposed roots dangling in the air) now thriving in its new location, we learn that plants are more resilient than we first thought, with a will to live that sometimes even overcomes our ignorance or mistakes.

I know many gardeners who, when selling their homes, have "dig rights" written into the sales contract. My friend Judy Glattstein had eighteen months to prepare for a move from Connecticut to western New Jersey, in which time she methodically lifted and potted thousands of woodland plants. "I'll be damned," Judy asserted, "if I'll let someone dig a swimming pool through my trillium!" For a while she and her husband owned houses in both places, and Judy made dozens of trips in a station wagon loaded down with plants and five-gallon buckets brimming with her homemade compost. When the Connecticut house was finally sold and moving day arrived, five wardrobe boxes holding shrubs too large to fit in the car were among the most precious cargo in the van.

Of course, a garden isn't a library of plants that can be transported, book by book, to be shelved in another location. A garden is the plants, the site, and all the interactions between them. But beyond this literal garden—beyond real time, real space, and real dirt—is a place we might call "the garden of the mind." The most transplantable parts of a garden are the memories, experience, and knowledge that we gleaned from it, all of which we carry with us in our hearts and souls, whether we move from place to place or stay planted in one garden all our lives.

LIFE IS TOO SHORT

My wealthy gardening friend Helen Stoddard always planted little trees. She planted a stick of a magnolia when she was seventy-five, and her friends shook their heads in disbelief. "Oh Helen," they chided, "why plant a small tree!" They were inferring two things: that Helen was frugal, but more, that she would never live long enough to see this tree in its glory.

Helen always pretended not to hear them.

I visited Helen shortly before she died of the cancer she had lived with for decades. I found her sitting on a garden bench, in the shade of that magnolia tree.

What if she had listened to her friends?

Often, when I want to plant something in the garden and come up with a dozen reasons why I shouldn't—"It's too late! You're too old! You'll never live to see it mature! It won't work there! Why bother?"—I think of Helen, and I give myself permission to do it. Not long ago, I bought a tree I had long wanted, *Sequoiadendron giganteum* 'Hazel Smith'. This is definitely a plant for future generations: if it ever reaches maturity, it won't be until the year 3000. But given another thirty years or so, it might achieve some stature, and if I am as lucky as Helen Stoddard and can still get around the garden then, I'll pull up a chair and relax in its shade. But I don't even need to wait that long. Already, 'Hazel Smith' has grown twice as tall as the day I planted it, and that makes me happy, right now.

Life is too short. So if we do what we want and if what we do is right and good, the future, like the trees, will take care of itself.

WIDE-EYED

All gardeners seem to be able to share their excitement about what might be considered a way of life. If gardening is not a religion, it is surely a consuming passion that has many loyal adherents. In an interview done for this book, Michigan landscape designer Tom Rooks spoke eloquently about his passion for nature and gardening:

"I was talking to a friend of mine who has a similar business, and we agreed that we can get sick of any part of it, but we never get sick of the plants. Every time I see something in bud about to come into flower, I'm like a little kid. Some things I look at are so beautiful, they make me dizzy, every time —it doesn't matter how many times I've seen them before. The great thing about this work is that you can never get old. I could be eighty years old and see those things and they will always seem new. I think gardeners tend to live longer lives, just because they can't stand *not* to see those bulbs they planted come into flower. They have to see what's going to happen next.

"And if you're a gardener and you do start losing it a little, it's hard to tell, because you're probably a little strange to begin with. It's great being a gardener—you can dress differently, act a little strangely, talk about things other people don't talk about, and it's almost expected of you. I don't know what I'd do if I had a job where I had to wear clean clothes, or had to play golf.

"We are very fortunate that way. I wonder, what do people do who are in love with things that are completely man-made? Like people who are in love with cars? What we're in love with is so complex and so never-ending, you can never feel you've done everything or learned everything about it. People who come to work for me sometimes get overwhelmed by the magnitude of it. I tell them, 'No, that's the great thing about this work. I've been doing it twenty-five years, and I'm still learning.' I have a friend who loves professional basketball, which I've never been into, and he was explaining to me all the complexities of the offense and the defense. And I could see it, but I still say there's no way basketball is as complex as bird migration, or the interaction of species in a rain forest.

"The downside is that rain forests are being destroyed since people aren't in love with them, or at least not enough people. But on the positive side, it's amazing how people respond right outside their own back doors when you make it friendlier for nature. The kids who see that, who knows what they'll do with it? It might just be a brief chapter in a young life. But it could change their lives forever."

Tom Rooks loves nature so much that he can barely stand to be indoors. He enjoys walking around his 60-acre property, ABOVE, through the meadows, by his ponds, and into the swampy woods, which he does on a boardwalk that zigs and zags beneath the trees, OPPOSITE. Rooks knows that part of the passion of a gardener is that "you can never feel you've done everything or learned everything."

MEMORIAL GARDENS

Gardeners are very aware of nature's cycles—the life and death of annuals, for instance, or the process that turns autumn leaves to leaf mold to plow into new garden beds. The preacher's "earth to earth, ashes to ashes, dust to dust" rings true to the gardener, especially one who makes compost. Dead plants nurture life, providing nutrients for a new generation of plants as well as food and shelter for animals and insects (as in a hollow tree or rotting log). Seen through the cycle of seasons and years, death becomes so much a part of life in the garden that the two are inseparable, one rolling into the other, as inexorable as the tides.

Death is also an inexorable part of human life, but being human, with human emotions, such losses of friends and loved ones can often be nearly impossible to bear. At such times getting out into the garden can help us cope, help us realize that our lives, and life in the garden, goes on even as we mourn. If the deceased was a gardener who shared favorite plants, an informal memorial might already be in place. In this sense, all our gardens are memorial gardens, full of plants that remind us of the people who gave them to us or introduced us to them, memories which become more poignant once that person dies.

Often a more conscious memorial may be planned—a planting or ornament or sometimes an entire memorial garden. I have mixed feelings about such memorials. At once they feel private and inaccessible, and then again, they can seem intrusive, such as one memorial consisting of a bronze casting of the dead person's foot. I feel better about a memorial tree than I do about such literal representations. Yes, death is part of the garden, but should dead people be part of it, too? Perhaps Victorian-era Americans were less squeamish about things like headstones in gardens. They created beautifully landscaped cemetery grounds, such as Mt. Auburn in Boston and Greenwood Cemetery in Brooklyn, New York, that became popular destinations for a Sunday stroll and were the de facto parks for the public in the days before public parks.

But after my father died, I decided to challenge my fears and apprehen-

sions and create a memorial to him in my garden. It wouldn't be "announced." There would be no plaque on it when I was through. But I would know what it was and who it was for.

While my father was dying of Alzheimer's disease, I could only marvel at the change the illness wrought. For most of his life he was a tower of silent strength, but in the end he was transformed, finding joy in things like kittens and bird songs, which he'd never seemed to notice before. He didn't say my mother's name, but he would do a little dance whenever he saw her, telling the world, "That's my girl!"

He didn't recognize me. "It's Ken," my mother would tell him, but he would just shake his head. This was not as upsetting as it might have been, because not being recognized, on some level, was the usual state of affairs between us. This was comfortable in his last years, when his disease removed the burden of history that keeps many parents and children apart, and he simply accepted me as a friendly face.

Ironically, a new drug my father took near the end of his life improved his mind, but also seemed to make him more aware of his condition. He didn't laugh or dance as much, and his physical health declined rapidly. In my last visits with him, by his side in a hospital bed, I offered to do things for him, and for the first time he accepted my help. At last I could give and he could take, and we became partners in a new relationship, man to man. I held his hand and talked. I pressed my forehead to his and he pushed back.

As I said good-bye on the day that turned out to be his last, he seemed startled for a second and stared deep into my eyes. "Kenny?" he asked, suddenly seeing beyond my grown-up body, my beard and bald head, and rediscovering the young son he loved. That was his last gift to me; and in those final days, his love also opened a gate that allowed our whole family to see each other with a new understanding and love.

Instead of dedicating a part of the garden to him, or planting a tree, I decided to make a piece of garden art. My mother's deepest memories seem to be linked to aromas—the smell of pot roast, the fragrance of flowers, especially the lilac. I planted two rows of these shrubs with a path between them, and made an ornamental gate for the entrance to this path, a reminder of my father's last gift. I often pass this memorial when I'm out in the garden, and often I don't give it a thought. But when I do, it is always a happy one.

A visit to a private memorial garden on Long Island begins with a walk beneath a rose-covered arch, OPPOSITE, past a birdbath usually filled with the sounds and sights of beautiful living things, and on to a quiet spot for contemplation. ABOVE: To remember my late father, I placed a gate made out of an old headboard at the start of the path between my lilacs. These flowers are my mother's favorites, and when they bloom, I think of both my parents.

YOU CAN TAKE IT WITH YOU

It's a horticultural truism to put the right plant in the right place. Sometimes we can create the "right" place in our garden by thinning branches above or amending the soil below, or by taking extreme measures—such as piling up rocks for a well-drained environment, or placing a rubber liner underground to simulate a bog. Another semi-truism that I follow goes "No plant is out until the third strike." If I want to grow some esoteric gem and it starts to decline, I analyze the environment before I give up on it.

Often I end up moving the plant to a new and, I hope, better location. For a novice gardener, digging a plant out by its roots seems a violent act, one with terminal consequences. But plants can be successfully moved—across the yard or across the country—using the right techniques and a little advance preparation. When I moved to the New Jersey garden, I made a nursery bed behind the house and plunked all sorts of plants from the Brooklyn garden into this space. I wanted them to grow to a good size so they could make an impact in the garden. I also needed time to figure out where they all might go. It took five years to completely empty this bed of all its plants, by which time some trees were more than nine feet tall.

When planning a move for a tree, consider root-pruning five or six months before—for example, in the spring for a fall move. Do this by plunging a spade to its complete depth in a circle at the "drip line," the imaginary line on the ground that relates to the spread of the tree's limbs above. Pruned

roots will branch, just as twigs do, creating a denser root system closer to the trunk that will come with the tree when it is moved.

If many roots have been lost, compensate for this by trimming the top growth. For instance, if a third of the roots are lost, prune a third of the branches or leafy growth. It is best to replant an uprooted tree, shrub, or perennial as quickly as possible. If the plant is in active growth, water it well and consider shading it and protecting it from wind with a burlap or sheer-fabric screen or canopy.

Many deciduous trees, which lose their leaves in autumn, respond best to planting in the fall, when they are going dormant. Although nothing is happening aboveground, stored sugars and starches are present in the roots, and new growth underground will continue until the soil is nearly frozen. For a big move or for a plant that has to be stored before replanting, herbaceous specimens can be potted and woody ones, if large, can be "balled and burlapped" (also called "B&B"), a process in which roots and soil are carefully excavated and a sheet of burlap is placed under the root ball, brought up on the sides, and tied around the trunk to make a sturdy package.

Most gardeners think of plants as stationary, but in fact they move—sometimes on their own, by windborne seed or creeping rhizomes, and sometimes with our help. ABOVE: I planted a few seeds from a Japanese maple in my Brooklyn garden—*Acer japonicum* 'Aconitifolium', with brilliant fall color—and when the sapling was fifteen years old, I dug it up, balled and burlapped the roots, and brought it to the garden in New Jersey, RIGHT.

Trees can also be transplanted by the "bare-root" method, when nearly all the soil is washed off the roots. At the planting site, the bare roots are carefully arranged over a mound of soil, covered with more soil, and watered thoroughly. Young deciduous trees planted bare-root often establish faster in the fall than B&B trees. One hint, which comes from sad experience: Never lift a B&B tree by its trunk. At best, this will break the fine feeder roots and set the tree back even further; at worst, the entire root ball may fall apart, leaving you with an unintended bare-root tree that will require intensive care to survive.

In many situations commercially available products can help reduce "transplant shock." Various "root stimulators" can help; the best are those containing vitamin B. Water-absorbent crystals, mixed with the soil used to backfill a transplanting hole, expand when wet and help keep moisture near the plant's root zone. Both these products help encourage the plant to put out new "feeder" roots to replace those lost during the move.

The old saying "Put a fifty-cent plant in a five-dollar hole" has been pretty much debunked, especially when it comes to planting trees, which can be killed by a well-meaning gardener who takes this advice to heart. If you dig a hole and fill it with richly amended new soil, two things happen. One, the tree will sink as the fluffy new soil settles. Two, the new soil will be held in the hole as if it were a container, and the tree roots will fill this container and may never venture beyond it. Eventually, like any pot-bound houseplant, the trees will suffer from stresses such as drought, low nutrition, root girdling and strangulation, and will die.

Dig the hole only as deep as the root ball is high. The "flare"—the place where the trunk meets the roots and widens—should end up at soil level. Lower the root ball into the hole and try not to move it once it is there. Remove as much as possible of the burlap, all the twine, and the metal basket, if possible. Fill the hole with soil, press it down, but do not step hard around the root ball, especially if the soil is moist, which will squeeze out the oxygen the plant needs. Pour several gallons of water into the hole. Let it all drain, and then fill with soil up to the flare. Frequent and thorough watering is crucial at this stage. Create a watering well by mounding soil into a circular ridge about two to three feet in diameter. The ridge will keep water above the transplant's roots, where it will slowly soak into the soil instead of running off.

Trees and other transplants also benefit from a coarse, open mulch, but keep the mulch about three inches away from the trunk. Avoid the common mistake of many landscapers, who love to surround a tree trunk with a neat circular mound of mulch several inches deep. Tiny roots grow into the mulch at the expense of the deeper new roots the tree depends on for long-term survival. Worse, rodents can make nests in the mulch and may chew away all the underground bark, killing the tree.

A LIFE IN THE GARDEN

Even on days when her arthritis flares like a swamp maple in autumn, Juana Flagg walks around her eleven-acre property in central Connecticut, to check on her trees. Juana has a sparkling personality and her delight for the life in her garden outshines any notion of infirmity. She is also a woman obsessed. For all her adult life, she has planted trees. Taking the walk each day through her property is like visiting her children, and she says it is never boring, always different. "I try to do it in the early morning," she says. "The serenity is wonderful, and there's a double joy: the joy of seeing something you see every day, and of seeing what new thing has happened since the day before. It's a rejuvenating feeling."

Juana Flagg has lived in the same house, on the same piece of land, since she moved there with her husband in 1956. Her four children grew up there, climbing the trees, making forts and hideaways beneath their branches. The trees became symbols of constancy and permanence for the children after their parents divorced, and even today, Juana is unable to have the carcass of a long-dead hemlock removed. A visitor might see this rotting tree trunk as an eyesore, but for Juana it is a reminder of more innocent times. "I can't bear to cut it down," she says. "My children played there."

The property that eventually became this beautiful garden was simply an overgrown, abandoned farm when the Flaggs moved in. Juana knew the land had potential, but at first couldn't see the trees for all the trees. Initially the garden was created by subtraction. Red cedars, shrouding the front of the house, were cut down, as was a privet hedge and ailing apple trees in a remnant orchard. A bulldozer took out an old tumble-down shed, a privy, and the blacktop playground area beside them. "Without doing anything but taking things away, it already looked better," she recalls.

From the old farmhouse, built in 1745, the property slowly slopes off through a large mowed meadow, past aged sugar maples and toward a grove of trees, most of them specimens of *Acer rubrum*, commonly called red or swamp maple. Beyond these trees was originally a swampy area. With the advice of state environmental officials, a small pond was carved out of it, which became a favorite recreation spot for the kids. To connect the marsh with the meadow, Juana made a path through the woods, which was the beginning of her woodland garden. She amended the soil between the maples, which allowed her to grow oakleaf hydrangeas and a variety of ferns and woodland groundcovers.

Juana created more formal garden areas close to the house, including flower and shrub borders, a walled garden around an in-ground swimming pool, and a vegetable garden that

Most people think fifty years makes an old garden, but for a gardener who loves trees, a half-century is simply a good start. The birch trees, PRECEDING PAGES, planted as nursery saplings, have grown enough to show the brilliant white bark of maturity. Between these trees, there is a glimpse of another plant of a certain age, the white wisteria standard. Juana Flagg has been able to watch her plantings soften the addition to her colonial farmhouse, TOP RIGHT. A swampy area, RIGHT, once a dense tangle of briers and brush, became a pond and now Juana can peer through the planted woodland understory and see the water's glow. In May, *Wisteria floribunda* 'Longissima Alba' is at its glorious peak, OPPOSITE.

she maintains meticulously, today with the help of Cruz Rivera, who shares her vigilant care for details. A small greenhouse allows her to grow seeds and cuttings, welcome tasks as age has taken its toll on her ability to do other chores. "I do things standing up most of the time," she says. "I can get down on my knees, but getting up is painful, which makes weeding very difficult. I use one of those kneelers, which has a pad you can kneel on, with handles to push yourself up, and then you can turn it over and sit on it. I couldn't do half the things I do without it." It is hard to reconcile the truth about the pains of a mature gardener when in the presence of this vivacious woman. In some ways, she seems like one of her beloved trees, which reach their greatest beauty after middle age.

The first new tree on the property—a Korean dogwood (*Cornus kousa*)—went in shortly after they moved in, and others quickly followed. The list includes white birches, sourwoods, several cherries, paper-bark maples, white pines, native dogwoods (*Cornus florida*), red oaks and pin oaks, shad-blows, tree lilacs, and single magnificent specimens of golden beech and fern-leaf beech.

"Come spring, I go to any of the nice nurseries around here, see what they've got and if I fall in love with a tree, I buy it, and then I

The plants surrounding the back of the house's addition include climbing hydrangea (**Hydrangea petiolaris**) over the door, a venerable cutleaf Japanese maple (**Acer palmatum**), shrubs, trees and even Japanese pachysandra (**Pachysandra terminalis**), a rampant grower, which Juana contained in a crisply edged bed. The dry-laid wall retains the earth of the swimming pool terrace, presenting more planting opportunities in man-made niches. A seed of royal azalea (**Rhododendron schlippenbachii**) sprouted in the wall. If left to grow, its roots might damage the wall, but Juana hasn't yet had the heart to dig it out.

Among Juana Flagg's most prized plants is a rarely seen fern-leaf beech, *Fagus sylvatica* 'Laciniata', ABOVE. A well-tended specimen such as this one keeps its lowest branches right to the ground. Although barely middle-aged, the tree exhibits all the character it will have at full maturity. The first sight of the vegetable garden is from the street, OPPOSITE, ABOVE, past lilacs and a small greenhouse. Viewed from the swimming pool terrace behind the house, BELOW, the true expanse of this mini-farm can be seen. Precisely planted raised beds within a split rail and wire fence contain flowers, herbs, and vegetables from peas to eggplants to rainbow Swiss chard.

figure out where to plant it," says Juana, who served for many years on her town's Urban Forestry Commission. In the spring of 2000 she planted a scarlet oak, which had been a long while on her "most wanted" list. "I'm afraid if I live to see it mature, this tree will be too close to a white pine," she says with a twinkle in her eyes. "But now my perspective has changed. I just turned seventy-nine, and if

I want to plant things too close, I think I can't be faulted if I leave that problem for my children."

During her childhood in Spain, Juana remembers accompanying her father to a mountaintop grove of beeches and playing among the trees while he gathered mushrooms. She moved to Connecticut in the autumn, and she fell in love with the colorful foliage of the maples. "Gardening with trees is a practical way of gardening," she says, "because, with luck, once you've planted a tree, all you have to do is watch it grow, and enjoy the feeling that you've—not really, but almost—created it. It always amazes me to think that many of the things growing here, I gave them their start, I helped them along over the years."

In her late fifties, after her children had grown up, Juana returned to school, studying

landscape design for two years at the University of Connecticut. "I did learn to work with some of the principles and elements of design," she says. "But my garden has taught me 90 percent of what I know. Most of what I've learned, I've learned here. A garden is the reflection of the person who made it, and who made hundreds of mistakes in the process."

She also continues to visit other gardens, and remains an active member of her local garden club. "There's no question we learn by seeing what other gardeners do," she says. "Then there are the serendipitous things, like the royal azalea growing out of a stone wall. It must have seeded itself there, and of course, if I had tried to do that, it never would have happened. It's breaking up the wall but it's so beautiful, I don't want to touch it."

Gardening is what keeps Juana Flagg looking forward, helping her stay young at heart and in mind. "Every year you think in terms of what's coming up," she says. "You go from one event in the garden to another, from moment to moment. April and May are perhaps my favorite months, and of course, October, and I love having the vegetables in the summer. Yet in the winter I can see the form, the skeleton of the garden, and by the end of March you can see the rosy haze of the red maples, so you know that things are coming back. There's something very vital about gardening. If I didn't garden, maybe I'd look at these things each year and wonder if, at my age, I would ever see them again. But I don't do that. I just can't."

One of Juana's favorite moments is when the flowering trees, such as the pink and white dogwoods, bloom across the great lawn. When asked about dandelions and other familiar lawn weeds, she shrugs off the critique, adding that the she prefers the yellow flowers to the chemical alternative.

FEAST FIRST

Many gardeners begin their careers with dreams of edible bounty, self-sufficiently feeding the entire family with the fresh, pesticide-free fruits and vegetables. Of all the horticultural pursuits, growing perfect produce could be the most noble, and the most difficult to master. As these gardeners discover that many of the fruits and vegetables they crave are available at the local markets, and growing food means welcoming all manner of animals to partake of the bounty, they often abandon the idea. They may then pursue other non-edible areas of horticulture, and learn the other way that gardens can feed us: through our souls.

Tom Rooks and Juana Flagg are two gardeners who have not given up on their dream (or need) to have fresh food from the garden. As passionate ornamental gardeners, they have also insisted that their vegetable gardens be beautiful as well. Anyone who tries growing food at home knows how hard it is to keep the critters away. Tom has succeeded in doing this in recent years, partly by continually fine-tuning his garden's defenses. Bags of hair and deer repellent hang from bamboo stakes in the corners of his beds. In her garden, Juana uses wire fencing to keep the bunnies at bay, its utilitarian nature concealed by a more ornamental split-rail fence.

Tom's vegetable garden sits on a sunny spot at the crest of a hillside above one of his ponds. Trellises and a sitting area have been incorporated into the design, making it a production garden as well as a place to relax and enjoy one of the most beautiful vistas on his property.

Juana's garden is in the typical New England

colonial style. The growing area contains rectangular beds that divide the garden space, and these beds are again divided for various crops and to provide access paths. At the center, where the paths converge, she summers one of her mature potted rosemary plants.

Both beautiful gardens include flowering plants. Tom grows cannas and other tropical perennials in and outside the garden fence. Juana's vegetables share the space with flowers for cutting, such as peonies in spring and cosmos in summer. Nearly a dozen varieties of roses grow outside and over the split-rail fence, with the hope that the thorns provide an added deterrent to hungry critters.

The centerpiece of Juana Flagg's formal vegetable garden is a **potted rosemary plant surrounded by *Zinnia* 'Profusion Cherry',** ABOVE. **Tom Rooks's fenced-in garden, OPPOSITE, is a centerpiece in its own right—the focal point of his landscape beside the old barn and at the crest of the hill overlooking one of the property's ponds.**

MR. NATURAL

As a child growing up in Grand Rapids, Michigan, Tom Rooks couldn't get enough of the natural world. "I feel like I was born with a love of nature," he says. "It's the only thing that's ever been my fascination." He was amazed when he saw a rabbit in his neighborhood of small city lots, and dismayed when developers filled in a tiny pond where he and his friends had found polliwogs. In his first attempt at gardening, he planted birdseed in pots on a windowsill, but the plants died when he tried to transplant them outside. To keep him from messing in his mother's flower beds, Tom's parents gave him a plot of his own. "It was a neat solution," he recalls, "giving a little kid ownership of something." He transplanted weed trees into his garden, box elders and Norway maples. "I tried to transplant dandelions," he says, "but they didn't take very well."

By age fourteen he was working for area landscapers, doing "real gardening," not just grass-cutting. By eighteen he was itching to go into business on his own, so he rode his bike around the neighborhood and stuck flyers in mailboxes. "By the time I got home," he remembers, "I had a message from a woman who is still a client, twenty-five years later."

Tom supported himself for two years of college with this landscaping work, hoping to get a degree in natural resources management. His romantic view of this profession— "I wanted to be out in nature, in the wilderness, helping the birds and the butterflies"— quickly caved in to the reality of the coursework. "It was all about timber harvests and

being a cop in a national park." A bit disillusioned, Tom took time off from school to figure out what he wanted to do, and discovered he was already doing it. He never went back to college, and while admitting that formal training in horticulture and design might have been "a shorter route to knowledge," he seems satisfied with the course his life has taken. "Most of my learning has been by touching

On an early summer morning, mist rises from one of the ponds Tom Rooks created on the grounds of his home, business, and nursery, PRECEDING PAGES. Tom kept the high-limbed old conifers in front of the house, ABOVE, when he bought and renovated this decidedly atypical Michigan bungalow (which may have come from a catalog). OPPOSITE: The trees framing the view from the porch seem more remarkable for having survived among farm fields, where woody plants are rarely spared. Beyond the grass lawn, a colorful perennial border hides the road but affords a perfect borrowed vista of neighboring fields.

and doing, by reading and asking questions," he says.

More than twenty years later, Rooks Landscaping employs forty-five at peak season, and Tom is surprised by his success and the size of his business. But no matter how much some parts of it frustrate him, he says he will never get sick of the plants. "I'll never let my business get big enough that I couldn't be hands on, designing gardens, handling plants."

Tom owns an Arts and Crafts bungalow that looks as if its builders traveled to California, fell in love with the style, and transplanted it to the mitten of Michigan. Over time, he has acquired adjacent properties and his holdings now total sixty acres. About half the land is devoted to nursery beds and polyethylene-covered hoop houses, and a quarter of the acreage leased to a farmer who grows alfalfa. Various gardens and several

man-made ponds make up the remainder of the property. When he moved into the house in 1988, both it and the land were in terrible condition. Raccoons and squirrels had made themselves at home in the attic, and frogs had taken up residence in the flooded basement. The property had been farmed badly, with the topsoil eroded and in some areas bulldozed off and sold. "I've done a lot of soil restoration," Tom says. "It's made me a firm believer that, if you keep adding leaf mulch and compost, you can really make a difference."

Clearing the overgrown brush around the house revealed several interesting trees. Tom chose to leave the mature pines standing in the front yard, and to highlight their best feature—the trunks with graphic patches of black and gray—by keeping the area beneath them open. The area behind the house is dominated by a giant box elder (*Acer*

negundo), which is likely older than the house. Beds of perennials line the road, effectively screening out passing cars but leaving open the vista of farm fields on the other side. A porch runs the length of the front of the house, which Tom has made more a place for recreation than a main entrance. Most people enter the house though the side garden, outside a kitchen addition and mud room, and to make this clear the area is planted with a tightly detailed perennial planting designed by Tom and a frequent collaborator, Steve Rosselet.

This precisely planned patch is the most decorative on the property: colorful mounds of grasses, herbs, and low shrubs, with tall conifers as exclamation points. The entry garden promotes a public face to the private house and serves as a "demonstration bed" for visitors and clients. The company offices are

A mudroom and kitchen addition has become the main entrance to the house, OPPOSITE. This planting, created with designer Steve Rosselet, serves as a demonstration garden for clients. The scheme is a low-maintenance arrangement of blue and mauve flowers and foliage—soft switch grass (*Panicum* sp.), floral spike from a *Yucca filamentosa*, wispy lavender Russian sage flowers (*Perovskia atriplicifolia*), the silver-blue foliage of a dianthus, dwarf conifers, feathery silver artemisia, and creeping hardy plumbago (*Ceratostigma plumbaginoides*). RIGHT: A hardy double sunflower (*Helianthus multiflorus*) grows in the perennial border along the roadside. OVERLEAF: In the wet meadow (LEFT), Indian plantain (*Cacalia atriplicifolia*) is a star. Another area (RIGHT) is more stylized; instead of only native plants, Tom has used a subtropical red-leafed canna.

in a garage building across the driveway from the house. Equipment, nursery pots, and bales of straw are stored in the old barn, which also serves as a dwelling for swallows. The birds swoop into the barn at dusk, flying low over the adjacent vegetable garden, which is another example of decoration, detail, demonstration, and utility. From this garden, there is a view of a low wet meadow, over which the sun rises in the summer.

The gardens farther away from the house become less formal, more free-form. The carefully placed perennial mounds and spiky evergreens give way to swaths and sweeps; well-clipped turf becomes a looser meadow. In a few places, Tom has planted great quantities of one or another native grass, such as switch grass (*Panicum virgatum*). These prairie-style plantings are actually aesthetic nursery beds. When plants are divided, the bounty is potted and readied for installation on job sites.

Past the *Panicum* hillside, the dry "prairie" blends into a meadow on a moister spot, and further on becomes a wet meadow. Large sweeps of a single plant give way to mixtures —first, of sunflowers, prairie coneflower, and

queen of the prairie, and then of milkweeds and cattail. A path winds through these stately plants, many of them as high as an elephant's eye. The effect is of an arching tunnel of tan and green, at the end of which is the first and most developed of the property's man-made ponds. Two chairs are set around a small campfire on the pond's shore, across from a naturalized planting of late-blooming daylilies. There is a dock in the pond, a tree-covered island, and a boardwalk leading to an old forest that floods and freezes over in winter, allowing Tom to ice-skate from tree to tree.

All of these elements can be viewed from the pond's most commanding feature—a screen house set just on a hill above the water's edge. This soaring wedge-shaped building, with a two-story screened wall made for the view, is Tom's retreat from the business that occupies much of the property and his time. "When you live where forty-five people work and clients tend to drop in, you need a place to escape," he says. "I don't linger long but typically I go out there every other day or so, usually at twilight. It's a way to watch the great variety of wildlife on the property and not be driven away by mosquitoes." A sleeping loft provides an opportunity for a more prolonged retreat. From there, a clear view is revealed of the treetops and sky.

Tom's design style is more naturalistic than native; he uses various grasses like Asian *Miscanthus* as well as his beloved local *Panicum*, and he has even planted (gasp!) bamboo. "We try to use natives as much as we can," he says, "But out here, people are still resistant to them. They say, 'Those are along the road.

Why would we pay you for that?' It's a process, and to take people along with you, you can't scare them too much. You need to show them good examples so they realize what the potential of these plants are." He has done public gardens, as well as several at office parks and country clubs. "If men see things planted in those kinds of settings," he says, "they'll be more likely to want them at home, rather than the ordinary: clipped yew, beds of a single variety of waxed begonia, perfect edges on green lawns, overly trimmed trees."

Only in recent years has Tom begun to reconcile native and natural on his own property. He is learning that the *Miscanthus* doesn't perform as well in his climate as the native *Panicum*, and though he likes the effect of bamboo, he has seen it slowly outgrow its boundaries and admits it will have to be removed. In his early years of garden-building, Tom dug into the edge of the wetland to build his ponds, but says he wouldn't do that quite so casually today. Now he is working to restore a relatively undisturbed area that runs through the center of the property. By removing the most problematic invasive plants, he hopes to create a natural corridor that will be a haven for the wildlife he has loved all his life.

Tom is constantly thinking of new ways to improve his sixty acres: areas to reclaim, meadows to plant, all aimed at making the property a more beautiful example of what can be done in that part of the Midwest. In the future, this should mean more plantings that feature local species, those that grew on the site before it was cleared for farmland. In some ways, he has become the "natural resource manager" he learned about in college, only on his own terms, on his own property.

With its gull-wing roof, the two-story screen house seems to **soar above the largest and most decoratively planted of the property's ponds, OPPOSITE.**

Among the remnants from the property's days as a farm are the barn and silo, OPPOSITE, where Tom stores equipment and a flock of swallows makes its home. This is where practical, old trees on the property have been pruned and renovated. ABOVE: The hillside below the vegetable garden is filled with native grass species in a field-style planting, complete with bluebirds and their houses. The field also serves as a nursery for Tom's landscaping business. RIGHT: Tom grows the perennial swamp sunflower (*Helianthus angustifolius*) between the pond and the screen house, where he sometimes sleeps on hot nights.

PART 2

PASSIONS

When I am interviewed for newspaper or magazine articles, reporters often ask me to name my favorite plant. Like a parent asked which child is the favorite, I find the question makes me squirm. To skirt this impossible choice, I often give my pat answer: "The next one I see." The question is unfair, even silly. Who could choose a single plant? My passions for plants—and in any area of gardening—are never constant, always changing, and always number more than one.

I could never pick the most special garden I've seen, either. I like different parts of many gardens, some of which I will remember until memory fails me. One such place is Roger Raiche's garden in Berkeley, California. Even though he rented his house (the former office and studio of the California Arts and Crafts architect Bernard Maybeck), Roger still packed the garden with thousands of species, including several of his own discoveries. The landlord insisted that the small patch of lawn in front of the house remain, so in protest one season Roger made an ingenious planting with an old reel mower propped up on one wheel. Spewing out the back of the mower was a symbolic froth of chopped turf actually made of flowering ornamental grass plants of various sizes. Another of my "perfect" garden spots was in New York State, where designer Hitch Lyman, working with owner Laura Fisher, placed a large antique fountain in the center of a circular garden room surrounded by a hemlock hedge. The garden was paved in smooth, river-worn rocks, perfectly set. Potted plants were placed on the edge of the fountain, and around a cast concrete set of table and chairs designed to mimic bark-covered logs and twigs.

Both these plantings are no more. Roger Raiche's lawn ornament was dug up after a year, and the lawn is gone as well, since, after six years as a tenant, Roger bought the house and now plants as he pleases. Laura Fisher moved elsewhere, to start another garden at another house. And yet, when asked to name my favorite gardens, these moments come to mind.

When it comes to favorite plants, the best is impossible to choose. Favorite what? Favorite annual? Perennial? Shrub? Tree? Groundcover? Fern? Moss? Favorite color of lichen? And with the ephemeral nature of plants, anything deemed the "best" disappears—not like the gardens gone by, but simply with the bloom times or changing seasons. One day as I walk through the garden, I call this or that special plant my favorite. The next day, another has taken its place. In autumn, my favorite shrub might be the one with the great fall color as the sun ignites its translucent leaves. A few weeks later, the best becomes a different shrub with brilliantly colored twigs. I am an equal-opportunity pushover.

My stock answer to those inquiring reporters is only partly tongue-in-cheek, because I am thrilled by the chase—discovering a new plant, in a book or someone else's garden, hunting for a source and, finally, acquiring it. Often, by the time I finally cross a plant off my want-list, I'm already searching for the next one.

Shopping for a new plant—or better yet, propagating it—is one of my passions. Working on detailed projects in the garden, fixing things and figuring things out—which, collectively, I consider "puttering"—is another. I have a knack for seeing problems and their solutions in other people's gardens. There is no doubt that we all become "garden blind," the point when we can no longer see the unfinished detail, the wrongly sited ornament, the dead end, or the missed opportunity. On a few occasions, I've been auctioned off as a garden doctor for fund-raising events, and I love that. I must admit that solving the same problems in my own garden takes much more work. Eyes are never fresh at home.

Among the many interesting puzzles posed by nature, the garden and plants, one that fascinates me is to try to determine the "cause of death." I'll go to great lengths—analyzing

In the late 1940s, Helen Stoddard received an unusual wedding present: the help of landscape architect Fletcher Steele to make a garden on the steep site of her new home in Worcester, Massachusetts. Steele designed a set of beautiful moss steps, PRECEDING PAGES, LEFT, which were actually a horticultural conceit: the real utility path was hidden behind the shrub to the right. After Helen's death the property was sold and the steps demolished, but they are now being re-created in her honor at the Tower Hill Botanic Garden in Boylston, Massachusetts, to which she was a generous patron. PRECEDING PAGES, RIGHT: Salvaged architectural terra-cotta ornaments are given new life in Bob Clark and Raul Zumba's garden in Oakland, California. OPPOSITE: Unlike other forms of art, gardens do not live forever. Laura Fisher's remarkable secret garden no longer exists but will survive forever in my memory. RIGHT: Roger Raiche created a memorable ode to a vanishing lawn—with ornamental grasses and grasslike plants spewing out of an old broken reel mower.

the light, air, water, soil conditions, inspecting the plants for any insects or diseases—to determine "whodunit." Botanical forensics is always enlightening. I've never lost a plant without learning something about its needs, and how to care for it better the next time.

RULING PASSION

When planning or refining a garden, it is important to consider what the garden provides for the people who use it. Your family may need a spot for recreation, perhaps a lawn for bowling or touch football. You may love outdoor entertaining, or simply want room to practice your horticultural art. Knowing what you'll need to satisfy your needs is hard to plan for, especially if this is an early garden in your career. Most often, the space dictates more about what your garden will be than your cravings and desires. But focusing on and promoting your passions will enhance the success of the garden, not just as a place of beauty, but for intellectual fulfillment and emotional satisfaction. Sometimes such a focus can actually reduce "maintenance," by which I mean doing the things we don't want to do (such as maintaining that lawn for someone else's game of touch football).

George Schenk, author of *Moss Gardening: Including Lichens, Liverworts, and Other Miniatures* (1997), admits that maintaining a moss carpet is more demanding in time and energy than a similar area of lawn. But this is beside the point, since a planted moss lawn is a garden, and grass lawn rarely is. The routine of mowing, feeding, and watering lawn is, for most people, a chore, but if your passion is moss, the time and energy spent cultivating such a space will yield pure pleasure.

Discovering your version of George Schenk's moss—your deepest, inner horticultural cravings—requires a kind of garden psychoanalysis, a task at

Niches and tiny microhabitats around your property can present **singular planting opportunities. This moist rock, ABOVE RIGHT, provides a home for ferns and moss. Growing moss can become a garden style and art form in its own right, as George Schenk described in his book on the subject. RIGHT: Carol Mercer created a wonderful moss planting around an arrangement of rocks that also serve as garden seats.**

which Rand Lee has become an expert in recent years. A garden lecturer and author of *Pleasures of the Cottage Garden* (1998), Rand has developed an exercise to help people "dream in detail" about the gardens they really want. "Yearning is essential to the gardening experience," he explains. "At the core of every garden dream are a few elements you can't live without, and unless you fulfill those desires, the garden will never be totally satisfying." In other words, it can be unsatisfying to have the most beautiful perennial border in town if what you really want is to eat a warm tomato fresh off the vine. This doesn't mean you can't have both flowers and vegetables and much more; only that, without the tomato juice dripping down your chin, the garden will seem incomplete at best, and drudgery at worst.

Rand calls the object of your affection the "ruling passion." To help find this focus, he has developed the "ruling passion exercise." It consists of jotting down elements of your dream garden in a variety of categories, then selecting the "ruling" element from each list. The morning I attended the Ruling Passion lecture, which Rand has given to thousands of gardeners all over the country, he focused on helping members of the audience come up with a "ruling garden use."

"You begin by listing all the uses to which you might like to put your ideal garden," Rand explains. "Remember, we are talking ideals here; don't edit yourself for reasons of practicality. Pretend money, time, and fitness are no object. What do you want a garden for? What do you want a garden to do for you?" For instance, if a ruling use was to be "a place to walk," it would affect the garden's entire design. There would be many paths, comfortably wide and smoothly paved. These paths would need destinations, and things staged to be encountered along the way, which could include some of the "ruling plants" or "ruling garden ornaments" that are discovered later in the exercise.

In making the "ruling" lists, speed is important, since we need to get in touch with the desires that lie beneath the surface, beyond the chattering of the rational mind. After spending a few minutes listing our uses, Rand suggests we each determine our "ruling use" by a simple process of comparing the first thing on the list with the second, then the more important of those two to the third, and on to the end. The stream of consciousness is very here-and-now, and taking the test a week later, or in a different gardening season, might yield a different result.

"This exercise threatens the fear mindset," Rand says. "It tells you to relax, start breathing, and imagine the kind of garden you'd have if you weren't afraid—of failure, of looking stupid, of your spouse getting mad at you, of doing it imperfectly. If you weren't afraid of joy."

You will not find true gardeners, people who know the power of the garden, choosing as their "ruling passion" to have a garden as a status symbol, to outshine the neighbors. You are the Picasso of your garden. Picasso seemed to ignore every convention, defied the scorn of his skeptics, and prevailed. So can you. In your garden, your domain, you are the only judge with a vote that counts. There may be competition—with your mate, perhaps, but more likely with yourself, because you will always want to grow and improve, to challenge yourself with new plants, new techniques, new ways of seeing.

EAST MEETS WEST COAST

Terry Welch is a landscape contractor and designer whose own home landscape, twenty miles northeast of Seattle, borrows inspiration from international sources: the eighteenth-century English Romantic movement; the indigenous woodland of the Pacific Northwest; and most of all, the gardens of Japan. His first professional horticultural career was with a lawn-mowing service in the early 1970s, while his earliest passion in gardening was to grow and tend bonsai trees. The lawn-mowing service grew into a complete design and contracting business, with the Japanese style emerging as the dominant influence.

Terry doesn't claim to have a Japanese garden (which can exist only in that country), but one made in what he calls the "Japanese aesthetic." His garden borrows and captures the essence, since he has studied and applied rigid Japanese principles of design, context, symbolism, and spirituality.

The plantings closest to his house are the most intricate, including a bonsai terrace where a wooden fence topped by tile serves as a backdrop and shelter for his precious dwarfed, potted trees. Further into the landscape, the constructions become more open and seemingly less refined. Finally, the garden melts into the woods and a fourteen-acre conservation easement with the town of Woodinville, Washington.

The 30-acre property was clear-cut in 1917. Ancient white cedars were felled to get to the tim-

Terry Welch began his gardening career with a lawn-mowing business and a few bonsai trees on a balcony. Today he is the owner of a large landscape design and installation firm in the Pacific Northwest. His collection of little trees grew as well, into a passion that provides both an escape from the pressures of work and the thematic style for some of his designs. His potted trees, such as the maples, ABOVE, live on a formal terrace, OPPOSITE, surrounded by a clipped yew hedge and a fence topped by roof tiles, and provide a diminutive counterpoint to the tall trees in the distance.

ber firs between them. Some of the cedars were dumped in low, wet areas on the property. Terry dredged the swampy places and unclogged the streams that feed them, creating two ponds and forming some of the dredgings into islands. He also discovered the hulking carcasses of the ancient white cedars preserved in the anaerobic muck.

Terry recognizes the Japanese belief in animism, an ideology in which every plant, rock, object, possesses a life force. The slowly decaying stumps of firs and cedars, some nearly five feet in diameter, have been respected like ancestors, left standing and naturally adorned with moss. Paths have been made to pass by these trunks, to pay homage in this free-form native "garden." The ponds and woods are reminiscent of an English landscape, with Terry's moon-viewing temple standing in for a folly, but the evergreens and mountains in the background lend an air that is at once Japanese and Pacific Northwest.

OPPOSITE, CLOCKWISE FROM TOP: The path to the house passes a covered temple bell, rhododendrons, and Japanese maples. A carved path into the wooded easement. Close to the house are combinations of formal dwarf evergreens beneath a stewartia tree. LEFT: A shelter straddles the spillway of the big pond and also marks the transition point from the planted gardens and the white cedar and fir woodlands around the property. BELOW: A rock with a depression that holds water symbolizes the concept of animism: that all things—rock, water, plants—have a life force. BELOW LEFT: The natural-looking swimming pool is sculpted with carefully placed rocks.

A NEW GARDEN

My ruling passion when I first took Rand Lee's test was "to see." I want a garden to present endlessly fascinating things to look at. With my desire to look and my need to putter in mind, I started a new planting in my New Jersey garden in 2000, a planting that would speak to the various facets in my gardening personality. I hoped it would be beautiful, to have something to look at in every season. I wanted it to be full of details, with nooks and crannies for little plants, interesting combinations, and a variety of conditions. I wanted it to be a space in which I could putter endlessly, if I liked, and one in which I could be comfortable when taking care of the plants, where I could either sit or kneel and not balance on one foot while stretching across forty-eight inches of bed.

And of course, I wanted more plants.

In the earliest drawings of the property, the sloping, sunny space behind the house (where we initially had a nursery bed) was marked with a U-shaped bed, drawn by extending lines out from the sides of the foundation of the house. A bend in the main branch of the river rounded the back of the land and suggested the arched shape for the bed, making it yet another circle on a property in which this geometric figure has become the leitmotif.

In my dream version of this garden, there would be a stone wall around the garden's perimeter, and gravel for the path and as a medium in which to grow a variety of coveted plants. Besides the beauty of such a structure, I wanted a wall in this sunny spot so it could be a heat sink—absorbing sunlight during the day and radiating its warmth back to the ground and plants in the cool evenings of late summer. I hoped that with the stones in the wall and the gravel in the soil, I might succeed in cheating the garden's Zone 6 a bit and grow borderline plants that might not survive elsewhere on the property.

My neighbor Chris Hagler is an expert stone-wall builder, and I peppered him with questions that summer. One day, perhaps as a challenge to himself (or to put an end to my questions), he offered to build the wall for me. He set only a few reasonable ground rules. My gardening partner Louis Bauer and I had to prepare the site and supply the stone for the wall, most of which was gathered from the property. And Chris insisted that once he began work, the design couldn't change. I had the idea to build a clay scale model, to work out the tricky details, such as whether the top of the wall would follow the grade or be level, and the places it would step down along its curving seventy-two-foot run. The model also served as a guide during construction, giving Chris a reference we all agreed on in advance.

Louis and I dug a trench for the wall's gravel base, and Chris started work on Labor Day weekend. To create pockets for plants, I filled black tube socks with soil and had Chris insert them at various spots as he was building the wall. He spent most evenings at the task, and part of each weekend. As he finished each section, he would exclaim, "It's yours now," and following right behind him, I would install the plants. By Veterans Day he was finished.

Although the new walled gravel garden does not receive as much sunlight as I would like, sun-loving plants thrived their first year in this well-drained, warm microclimate. In January, while the soil in the rest of the garden was frozen solid, I was still able to plant bulbs in the unfrozen, gravelly soil next to the wall. And with the reflective warmth, a few marginally hardy plants, including euphorbias and *Crocosmia*, came through the first winter unscathed. The first tiny bulbs appeared in February and March, and there was something glorious and interesting in the space up until the first frost and beyond. Hardy cyclamens, grown from seed, bloomed in August and continued for months. Their gorgeous mottled and marbled green and silver leaves are visible when the snow melts from the gravel bed, and were still pretty in late spring until the plants finally fell into summer dormancy.

When my neighbor Chris Hagler agreed to build me a 72-foot-long dry stone wall, I made a model of the project, OPPOSITE, to make sure the wall would be right the first time. The six-week project began with digging a trench in the footprint of the wall, which was filled with two feet of crushed stone. As Chris placed the stones, ABOVE, I installed long black cotton socks filled with soil, angled toward the ground. As he finished each section, he turned it over to me for planting. Nearly all the stone came from the property, and the artisan's fee was equally inexpensive: occasional gourmet dinners (and frozen margaritas) for him and his wife, Jill.

The bed was made by tilling gravel with the clay fill on the site and a bit of compost. The mix is nearly 50 percent gravel, and is about a foot and a half deep. The path areas are six inches of pure gravel. The first thing planted, even before the wall began, was a single columnar yew. Another permanent shrub is a variegated boxwood, which will be trained into an urn shape as a nod to "The Rosarie," at Willowwood Arboretum. That garden's centerpiece is a giant Italian oil jar. I couldn't afford an antique, but thought it would be fun to trim the shrub in the old jar's honor.

I think about how much pleasure this new garden brings me, and imagine that if I could only have one garden (perish the thought), or for some reason could only manage one garden spot, the gravel garden would be it. My worry is that every weed in creation will love this garden as much as I do. Weed seeds find the nooks and crannies of gravel ideal for germination: picture the edge of the sidewalk, and the spaces between bricks, and multiply that by the tens of thousands of spaces between the gravel mulch on the garden's beds and the path around the inside of the wall. So far, so good. I didn't plan this as a low-maintenance garden, but it is. The few weeds that appear in the gravel are easy to see and remove.

When my mother came to visit in the gravel garden's first spring, she donned a large straw hat, sat in a chair with a tray of propagated *Sempervivum*, hen-and-chickens, in her lap, and used a probing tool to work a dozen or so of these plants between the stones of the wall. Watching her, I saw a vision of my own future, or at least one possible version of it. If the various aches and pains I now feel ever begin to really slow me down, I may have to learn to focus my passions, simplifying other areas of the garden in favor of the ones that I can handle and that give me the most pleasure.

At that point I can see myself concentrating on the gravel garden, puttering and playing in this small yet detailed space. Years from now, I might be found sitting in a chair, my head covered with a straw hat, as I poke plants into the spaces between the stones in the wall.

At "The Rosarie," a feature of the Willowwood Arboretum in a neighboring county, a large birdhouse overlooks a gravel-path planting, with an antique Mediterranean oil jar, TOP. I paid tribute to this garden by making a topiary jar out of clipped boxwood (*Buxus sempervirens* 'Elegantissima'), OPPOSITE. The long wall, shaped like a backward question mark, can clearly be seen in the winter snow, ABOVE.

PLANT EXPLORATION

Who would have guessed that one of the fantasy careers of the new century would be a revival of one from centuries past: plant exploration. Great wealth once came from the discovery and importation of medicinal and culinary herbs. The search for spices led to the formation of the great trading companies of the Dutch and British. The breadfruit of the *Bounty* and tales of missionary heads on stakes populated literature and lore. Ornamental plants were popular, too. In the colonies, William Bartram's expeditions were funded by European subscribers eager to grow flowers from the New World.

The last great hunter of the Age of Plant Exploration was Ernest Henry Wilson, who walked with a limp through much of his life—a reminder of a broken leg suffered in a landslide in China, after which he had to be carried for twenty days to the nearest medical outpost. Wilson was a romantic, dashing figure, much like the real-life T. E. Lawrence (of Arabia) or the more recent cinematic creation, Indiana Jones. In all, Wilson brought back 100,000 specimens of more than 5,000 species, and 60 plants were named for him. Like Lawrence, Wilson survived his exploits, only to die closer to home. He was killed in 1930 in a car accident in a Boston suburb.

Plant exploration in the late twentieth century focused on medicinal plants, again, with researchers trying to stay a few steps ahead of the loggers and bulldozers in the rain forests of Central and South America. The desire to find garden plants was also revived, and again turned to Asia. Barry Yinger explored Japan and Korea, refusing to set foot in China for political reasons. Today, the focus is again on China and west to Nepal. The explorer of this century is Daniel J. Hinkley. Since 1980 he has made many trips to Asia to collect plant material (mostly seeds) that he propagates for his Washington State garden and nursery, Heronswood.

Dan's interest in plants is lifelong, but he cites as a "pivotal moment" a trip he took with a friend and a dog when he was a nineteen-year-old sophomore at Michigan State University. They went to search for what was reported to be the last virgin stand of the eastern white cedar (*Thuja occidentalis*), growing on an island in northern Lake Michigan. "After three days of searching, we finally found this small old-growth stand," Dan wrote in his 1999 book, *The Explorer's Garden*. "It was an electrifying experience."

The gardens at Heronswood carry on this theme. It is a place to see new plants for private gardens and to be overwhelmed by the way they are displayed, tended, indulged, and revered. When opportunity permits and the garden is open, as it is on certain dates and by prearrangement, a visitor can explore this magical place and discover species unknown to the horticulture of one's own backyard.

Dan Hinkley is a modern plant explorer whose discoveries go first to his Heronswood Nursery in Kingston, Washington. There, collected seeds are germinated and grown in the rich soil of the Pacific Northwest garden, ABOVE, along with plants such as the variegated giant dogwood (*Cornus controversa* 'Variegata') beside a folly created by George Little and David Lewis. Among Hinkley's most popular finds are Asian Jack-in-the-pulpit relatives, such as a form of *Arisaema consanguineum*, OPPOSITE.

PASSION FOR NATIVES

The Hamptons, on the eastern end of Long Island, New York, are the playgrounds of the rich and famous. Celebrity CEOs and movie moguls schmooze at posh watering holes. Mansions sprout like mushrooms, sometimes out of the dust of former mansions judged too small or too old for the newcomers. Everyone *has* a garden, but few people garden.

Franklin Salasky breaks the East Hampton stereotype. His "mansion" is a renovated shingled shack on a quarter acre, on what some might consider the wrong side of the tracks. And if you visited Franklin's garden, in what is locally known as the Village, you wouldn't feel you were in town, and especially not this bustling resort community. It does what all the best gardens do: it takes you away from everything, whisks you into its own special environment, providing a great sense of the natural habitats and flora of Long Island.

Franklin is a New York City–based architect and partner in B5 Studio. His little weekend house is exquisite, as one would expect from someone who produces interiors for well-heeled families. Not much of the original house is immediately evident, and that can be said for the landscape as well. What wasn't lost during the installation of a basement under the house or taken when he had the driveway moved to give him more privacy was removed intentionally when he turned his attention to the property. The house and garden were not restored or renovated; instead, they were newly designed to conform to Franklin's strict ideas about what both should be.

The house is a seaside dream, even though there is no view of the Atlantic Ocean. The building is like a Transformer toy: from a tight little drum centered around a wood stove in the tall-ceiling living room, it turns inside out and becomes an open beach house where salt air, sunlight, and guests circulate as freely as the breeze. The living room has one wall of bi-folding doors that open into a narrow screened walk, which leads from the official front of the house to the dining room door at the back. Every room, even the master bath, has a door leading outside, and all windows have wonderfully framed year-round views of the garden.

As Franklin started to think about what kind of garden he wanted, the possibilities seemed daunting at first. He wanted it to be a comfortable, usable space for entertaining, but admits to having "zero" experience as a gardener. He began where many people do: "I looked at pictures, I looked at other gardens," he says. "I saw lots of plants I loved, and soon I came to love so many pretty things that I was totally confused."

The usual response for a novice gardener, faced with infinite choices, is to take a little of this, a little of that, and create a hodge-podge of a garden. But Franklin approaches all of his jobs with a scholarly, persistent

Architect and interior designer Franklin Salasky converted a small house, PRECEDING PAGES, in the beach community of East Hampton, Long Island, into an ideal weekend home with an equally ideal and manageable garden. The program for the garden was very specific: all plants would be limited to those that originated on Long Island. The main entrance to the house is from a paved dooryard garden, OPPOSITE, featuring orange American turk's-cap lily (*Lilium superbum*), RIGHT, dogwood, viburnum, and the property's leitmotif: fragrant sweet pepperbush (*Clethra alnifolia*).

intent. If he wants a historical decoration for a room, for example, he researches that style. Since he was on Long Island, he researched Long Island native flora, one of the things that attracted him to East Hampton in the first place. One day he heard a local naturalist speak about the importance of preserving native plants in gardens (an idea that had first come to his attention a few years earlier, when he read *The Natural Habitat Garden*).

"My friends and I were lamenting the fact that the native landscape was disappearing

before our eyes," he recalls. "I love this landscape, and I loved the idea of doing something restorative in my own garden." He knew it would just be a small gesture—nothing more was possible on such a small lot—but thought the idea was challenging and might encourage others to do the same.

He also knew that he couldn't do this project by himself. For one thing, the plants he read about and saw in nature were not available in area garden centers and nurseries. He hired Betsey Perrier, a local landscape designer and native plant expert, who provided the expertise he needed to execute his wildest dreams.

"Not all my clients want native plants," Perrier explains. "But of the many who do, Franklin is the only one who got into it philosophically, to the extent that he only wanted Long Island natives, not just U.S. natives or East Coast natives. He wanted the plants to be native to *here*." More common, she says, are new clients who announce at their initial

*In a nod to the seaside neighborhood, Franklin bought a folksy concrete seahorse, ABOVE, and installed it near the screened-porch entry to the house. OPPOSITE: The porch, facing a small lawn, chairs, and plantings, also serves as an arbor for Virginia creeper (**Parthenocissus quinquefolia**) and orange trumpet vine (**Campsis** sp.). OVERLEAF, LEFT: Franklin used the back wall of his neighbor's shed as a backdrop for a bluestone-paved seating area beneath an old maple tree. RIGHT: One of the garden's water features is a rubber-sheet-lined wooden trough where plants such as pickerelweed bloom.*

meeting: "The first thing I want you to do is get rid of all the weeds." She has to inform them gently that those "weeds" are the same native plants they have hired her to put in.

"I told Betsey I wanted to make a garden that had a contact with, and was connected to, the landscapes around it—the landscapes that are almost gone," Franklin recalls. "I had been to nearly every preserve and protected site, and I thought they were beautiful, especially the way the plants come in contact with each other—for example, the way a *Clethra* grows up through a bayberry, winds through it and uses it for support. I wanted to create some of that on my property."

With a few exceptions, everything found in Franklin's garden is native to eastern Long Island. "A lot of them are the plants we see around, or could see around," Franklin says. "A lot of them really are as common as weeds. When we look at an undisturbed part of the landscape, these are the plants. And while the palette is very limiting, it seems to me that the success of gardening is in limiting the palette."

Imagining this spot as a blank slate belies the actual condition and the amount of work that had to be done to implement the plans. The outer edges of the plot had been smothered in Oriental bittersweet (*Celastrus orbiculatus*), a fruiting vine from Japan that cloaks neglected wood lots on Long Island like kudzu does in the Southeast. Franklin has discovered over the years that construction outdoors is different from construction indoors. Tearing down an interior wall is unpleasant work, at best, but at least it doesn't grow back, as the bittersweet tries to do. Over time, areas were cleared, prepared, and planted.

Franklin wanted the various parts of his garden to flow together as seamlessly as the rooms in his little gem of a house, which he worked on for nearly ten years. As an architect, he was able to design these outdoor spaces himself, but he needed Betsey's skill to help him populate those rooms with appropriate plants. "We would discuss what effect he wanted in each place, and what plants would work in them," she remembers. "They were small areas, and he didn't want a million different plants." Annuals for seasonal color are planted in discreet pots, as are a few herbs and salad greens.

The criterion also allowed for cultivars of local plants (selected varieties that have been put into cultivation). One is *Clethra* 'Hummingbird', smaller than the species and less likely to be floppy in shady areas. Other plants in the garden include a stand of *Aronia arbutifolia*, which shares a bed with just four other species: hay-scented fern, dogwood (*Cornus florida*), lowbush blueberry (*Vaccinium angustifolium*), and Virginia creeper (*Parthenocissus quinquefolia*). A large specimen of staghorn sumac, *Rhus typhina* 'Laciniata', grows in one corner of the property, a few red maples grow in another corner. *Viburnum dentatum* and *V. trilobum* are used as a screen at the end of the driveway. A small stand of shadblow (*Amelanchier canadensis*)

Woody plant guru Michael M. Dirr wrote in his seminal work, ***Manual of Woody Landscape Plants***: "A garden without a viburnum is akin to life without music and art." Franklin has taken these words to heart, growing examples of several local species, including American cranberry bush (***Viburnum trilobum***) planted to screen the parking area from the house, OPPOSITE, BELOW. Besides flowering, these disease-resistant shrubs produce an abundance of fruit for the birds into the autumn. OPPOSITE, ABOVE: Trumpet vine adorns the shed's garden wall. Franklin hopes that the confined planting, next to the building, will help curb the vine's aggressive tendencies.

provides snow-white blossoms in the spring and, along with many of the plants on the property, food for wildlife and great fall color. At Betsey's recommendation, a drip irrigation system was installed, which helped the plants get established and now helps them thrive in spite of the area's hot, dry summers.

Part of Franklin's plan was to open up the view into a wooded reserve across the road. The vista is not endless, but serves as a visual buffer and outer area screen. It also enlarges the apparent garden, by borrowing neighboring plants and suggesting that the ocean or acres of woods lie just beyond the pergola area. Capitalizing on possible scenery advantages is a good idea in any garden, but especially in one as small as this.

Franklin loves his native garden, as much for its uniqueness as anything, and appreciates the palette that limits acquisitions. He is still coming to terms with the fact that the outdoor rooms will not be static. He wants and welcomes change and growth, but finds the surprises a little disconcerting. The Zen of weeding is a devotion he has yet to cultivate.

Many people reject the possibility of an all-native garden because they perceive it to lack flowers and color, but Franklin has learned that this isn't the case. In spring his garden is full of color, from woodland wildflowers and the new growth and flowers of the trees and shrubs. In the summer, the garden's beauty is subtle, but the design is so well thought out—the effect as soothing as the sound of waves breaking on the beach—that few people notice that the plants are native, or even mostly green. The garden looks its best during the drawn-out Long Island fall, with the foliage of various plants changing color at different times. "There is a whole range of reds, and browns," Franklin

says. "And then you have the twiggy structure of the plants after the leaves drop. You have to appreciate structure if you're going to go into natives." The tans and gold of dried foliage remind us that brown is a color, too, and when struck by the long rays of winter sunlight, these leaves seem to glow from within.

Franklin says that his friends were shocked that the garden worked as well as it did. "They tried to talk me out of it. They said things like 'Why do you want to be so restrictive? Why don't you have more pretty plants? be more artful? have more color? be more conscious of placement or juxtaposition? Why couldn't you have a daylily if you think it's pretty?'

"Maybe I will. But I didn't want to run around looking at every single plant in the world that was for sale. Betsey gave me a list and that's what I went by. If I had a shady area, I knew I could use these plants. In a sunny area, I could use those plants. In a sense, it's a very great simplification. If you don't know how to cook everything well, isn't it better to stick to something simple?"

In winter, the last of the *Viburnum trilobum* fruits dangle from the shrubs, OPPOSITE, before being eaten by migrating birds. Other shrubs grown in the garden for fruit and spectacular autumn color are deciduous lowbush blueberry (*Vaccinium* sp.), and red chokeberry (*Aronia arbutifolia*). ABOVE RIGHT: The inkberry (*Ilex glabra*), with jet-black berries, is nondescript in other seasons but a standout when seen against a backdrop of snow. RIGHT: By the end of the season, as grasses turn golden and the fiery colors of the sumac begin to fade, the blue color of the house is especially effective. On just a fifth of an acre, Franklin has brought together all elements for the perfect outdoor living space.

MOVING WATER

Franklin Salasky's garden and the one developed by Bob Clark and Raul Zumba (see the following profile) might seem to have very little in common. And yet, in a way, both of these creations are products of their environments. Franklin devoted his garden to the east end of Long Island, New York, and the indigenous flora it supports. Bob and Raul developed their garden in artistic and atmospheric conditions unique to the Bay Area, east of San Francisco. The influences are different, but the landscapes have even more in common. Both have developed their sites into distinctive "rooms," and both gardens also welcome water.

Nothing is as completely entrancing as water in a landscape, but few other garden features demand more attention than a fountain, pool, or pond. When you read catalogs or hear descriptions about adding a water feature, be prepared to project into the future. When the catalog reads "dig a hole," imagine the task. Even a small pool, 10 by 10 feet and three feet deep (which is enough to overwinter fish and a water lily in a cold climate) equals 300 cubic feet of soil to be moved, not to mention the rocks and roots that may be encountered along the way.

The water features are differently made in the two gardens, but the effects are similar. In Franklin's case, the water fills geometric shapes. A small round pool by the entrance to the house was made with a stock tank, sunk in the ground, and a raised

rectangular pool is actually a wooden trough lined with a butyl rubber sheet. These water features are like holes in the earth, deep eyes set into the landscape, introducing an implied vertical line—piercing down through the earth's surface and then shooting up to the sky—that contrasts sharply with the horizontal plane of this coastal garden. These pools also echo the ocean, just a few blocks away, and are a reminder of the cooling effects of water on summer days when the air temperature climbs into the 90s.

The major water feature in Bob and Raul's garden, a small pond nearly at the center of the terraced hillside, presents a different feel from Franklin's pools. There is no need to cool visitors in a climate where summer temperatures rarely top 80°F, but the water soothes in other ways. The sky may not be open to reflect on the water surface, but the pool is a place for reflection of the emotional kind. This contrivance, surrounded by a wide variety of plants and sculpture, creates a spot that transports the visitor away from notions of everyday life.

Both gardens also use the refreshing and comforting sound of moving water. At Bob and Raul's, water drips gently down a rock construction. Franklin's front pool has a bubbler that adds a gurgling sound to the entry space.

Whether moving or still, water adds a dimension to the garden. **Still water captures the sky and brings it down to earth. Moving water supplies sound to this sight. The small round pool in Franklin Salasky's dooryard garden, OPPOSITE, made by burying a galvanized stock tank in the ground and lining it with a butyl rubber sheet, appears deep, like an eye that affords a glimpse into the soul of the garden. The success of this feature encouraged Franklin to add a raised rubber-lined wooden pool behind the house. ABOVE: On most summer days, one or two water lilies open at dawn.**

Bob Clark and Raul Zumba also recognize the special effect of water, which they use throughout their hillside

garden, OPPOSITE. The largest pool blends into the landscape and serves to create a seemingly private outdoor room where a visitor is isolated from the rest of the garden. Trees and shrubs overhang the pool, softening its edges and allowing the water's source, a grotto-like construction of rocks, to seem completely natural. Other water features include simple vessels of plain water, LEFT, and a planted bowl with a 17th-century Buddha, BELOW. When added to a pond or ornamental pool, nontoxic dyes available from water-garden supply sources make the liquid appear black and endlessly deep, and containers or pools bottomless.

PASSION PLAY

The danger in overpopulating a garden is that the result becomes a polka-dot mess featuring one of everything. But a group of gardeners in the San Francisco Bay Area called The Hortisexuals dismisses that restricting notion. They take as their motto "No plant is safe," and fill their gardens with the multitude of plants that thrive in the area's near-ideal climate. And their acquisitiveness is not limited to living things. Many forms and styles of sculpture, along with flatware and tea cups, bowling balls, dime-store ornaments, and rusted dumpsite finds—all this jostles for space with the plants, filling every nook and cranny. The word "junkyard" might come to mind, but in reality, these gardens are spectacular. Perhaps their motto should be "Nothing succeeds like excess."

In order to be successful, a garden that pushes the envelope and then bursts its seams needs good design and structure. No one knows this better than Bob Clark, who, it could be said, holds up the aesthetic standard for The Hortisexuals. Some fifty works by area artists and thousands of plants fill his own garden, created with Raul Zumba on a steeply sloping acre in the hills above Oakland. Bob is one of the area's most sought-after garden designers. Raul, a former nurse, now designs gardens as well.

Many of Bob's designs for clients are formal, but his playfulness and theatricality are evident in these landscapes, which are part estate garden, part Chelsea Flower Show. His first gardening job was for a wealthy Oakland family, and they gave him free rein in their

A steel gate by sculptor Mark Bulwinkle, covered with white potato vine (*Solanum jasminoides* 'Album'), ABOVE, greets visitors to the Oakland, California, property and leads to the first garden space, made atop the original driveway, PRECEDING PAGES. Although it is impossible to imagine what lies ahead, many of the landscape's elements make introductory appearances: brick walls built by Raul Zumba, sculptures, and plants, plants, plants. A large shrub, beside the path leading behind the house, turns out to be a topiary creature—maybe a dinosaur or prehistoric bird. OPPOSITE: Piercing a creeping fig-covered brick wall, another arched gate leads from the formal lower rose garden to the cactus plantings on the side of the house. It announces, in a tribute to Gertrude Stein, exactly where a visitor has arrived: "There."

one-acre English-style garden. "I got spoiled early on," he says. "I got to learn my craft in an ideal situation, because I could be experimental, they allowed me to fail. That's still a theme of my work, in the sense that today, as a designer, I never do a garden where I don't try something I haven't done before." This doesn't mean that he doesn't do what clients want, only that he always tries to add his own twist or flair.

Among the mirror-image houses, lawns, and foundation plantings of the neighborhood, Bob and Raul's property stands out like a fantasy island. When they bought it in 1989, most of the plantings had either been trampled or eaten during its former incarnation as a llama farm. On this once-barren acre, surrounding a typical ranch house, they have created an unabashed tribute to art, color, and whimsy, all of which is evident even from outside the garden. The numbers of the street address ripple down the spine of a dragon/mailbox (by garden designer and sculptor Ralph Barnes), and if that hint is missed, a pair of tall swinging gates, featuring chortling cartoon faces drawn in recycled steel (by sculptor Mark Bulwinkle), confirms that this is a magical place. The writer and art collector Gertrude Stein once said of Oakland, "There is no there there." But emblazoned across the top of an arched iron gate in the garden is a word that lets visitors know where they have arrived: "There."

The steep hillside has been cut into terraces that are held by Raul's fanciful brick retaining walls. In the gentle Bay Area climate, garden constructions of brick and concrete do not need to be as strong as those built in areas of the country subject to periodic freezing and thawing. This gave Bob and Raul the freedom to have some of the walls

undulate in waves, and others to be pierced
with holes or have wine bottles embedded in
them for "windows." Even more fanciful are
Raul's couches, made of concrete studded
with glistening mirror fragments, pottery
shards, and marbles.

The climate also suits a remarkable range
of plants. It is arid enough for Mediterranean
species such as salvias and rosemary, warm
enough for the garden's bountiful grapefruit
tree, hot enough for hibiscus and bougainvillea, but cool enough for plants like flowering
cherries, which need a chilling dormant season to bloom. Both gardeners have a passion
for voluptuous tropical plants, Raul remem-
bering them from his native Ecuador. "There
were wild tangles of plants," he recalls, "trees
full of bromeliads and orchids."

Some of the sculptures nestle into the surrounding growth, which sometimes threatens
to upstage them. The sawtooth-edged leaves
of *Melianthus major* attract more attention
than the brilliant silver gazing globe tucked
among them. Trellises, Roman columns, and
totem poles come into view among plants
such as the treelike *Brugmansia aurea*, which
bears scores of enormous dangling yellow
trumpets. From a towering brick planter
sprouts a cascading *Loropetalum chinense*
'Plum Delight', whose garnet leaves sparkle
with cherry-red, ribbonlike flowers. Beneath

A path on the hill passes a concrete couch studded with
mirror-shards, marbles, and broken tile, OPPOSITE,
that no visitor can resist sitting on. ABOVE RIGHT:
Further along, the path turns to reveal a vista that
serves as a reminder that this is actually a backyard—
on earth—with a view of the house's roof and hills in
the distance. RIGHT: Plants next to the house include
the chartreuse flower heads of *Euphorbia characis*
'Wulfenii' with gray-green *Melianthus major* leaves,
a silver gazing ball, and the yellow trumpet flowers
of *Brugmansia aurea*.

Paths lead everywhere: to the top of the property and a view of San Francisco Bay, RIGHT, and in the opposite direction, the path's edge covered by arching grasses and grasslike plants, BOTTOM RIGHT. A brick walk near the lawn and rose garden is, in keeping with those traditional plantings, lined with tulips, CENTER, in spring. One of the most arresting pathways, OPPOSITE, is made of stepping-stones planted with golden pearlwort (*Sagina subulata* 'Aurea').

it, *Salvia mexicana* 'Tula' (also called 'Limelight') sports royal blue flowers that dart out from chartreuse calyxes.

Steps (rather than llama tracks) now climb the terraced hillside, to paths that meander through a series of distinct rooms, each planted in a different style, and each of which is obscured from view until you duck around a corner, when the next tableau is revealed. These rooms include a sunny rose garden, a quiet woodland glen with a floor of chartreuse moss and glistening moist black rock, a lush water garden with a round pool and waterfall. Having separate rooms makes the experience of walking through the garden captivating, since you never know what you might find next. The rooms also serve to highlight the artwork. If fifty sculptures were viewed at once, the garden would look like a shop, or worse; but in this framework of special "galleries" and perfect settings, each one gets to shine. The pool garden, for instance, has as its focal point a bronze goddess, sculpted by Michelle Muennig. In another bed, a gigantic granite head carved by Marcia Donahue rests in quiet repose, creating a soothing counterpoint to the spiky swordlike leaves of New Zealand flax (*Phormium tenax*). Elsewhere, Donahue's anatomically inspired *Bone-boo*, made from bone-shaped segments of colorful glazed pottery threaded over steel rebar, garners all the attention.

In one area of the garden, Bob and Raul

commissioned Bay Area gardener Archie Days to create a room using cacti and succulents: this might just be the garden's most remarkable display. The medium was a good choice, since the plants will be slow to outgrow their arrangement. In one corner of this space, beneath a bower of pale yellow *Pandorea pandorana* flowers, Days managed to erase the line between sculpture and plant. He assembled a chorus of prickly pears (*Opuntia* sp.) in pots, cutting out little singing "mouths" from their spiny pads (which, as extreme as it sounds, does not hurt the plants). Such an unconventional cacti chorus seems normal here; the more traditional areas, such as the croquet court carpeted with lush lawn, are the ones that seem discordant in this fantasyland. But even there, with gracious wide steps leading to the greensward flanked by pots of flowers that change with the season, Bob gives the scene a tweak. Instead of providing a traditional teak or wrought-iron garden bench for spectators watching the game, the furniture here is another of Raul's concrete, shard-studded sofas.

Incorporating these remarkable and often eccentric creations might be the best example of Bob and Raul's artistry. Along with sculpture by known artists are flea-market finds, recycled rubble, broken crockery and ornaments, and antiques such as a seventeenth-century Buddha. The plantings are lush and exotic-looking and, at their best, are slightly out of sync with the seasons. "To me, the garden is at its most beautiful in the fall, because it seems nothing like fall at all," Bob says. "In November we might have *Cestrum elegans* blooming over *Melianthus major,* and the abutilons are at their peak—all of them plants not usually associated with that time of year."

This is a garden of layer upon layer: the

more you look, the more you see. And like all good gardens, those layers are always changing, sometimes subtly and other times, depending on the prevailing whims and wishes of the gardeners, drastically. Bob has recently developed an obsession with Japanese maples, and is becoming more interested in cultivating a woodland look in parts of the garden. He is doing some experimental pruning: for example, limbing up a Harry Lauder's walking stick (*Corylus avellana* 'Contorta') into a tree, or using formal topiary training to create surreal shapes in a Coast redwood (*Sequoia sempervirens*).

"I run on a lot of different tracks at the same time, as you can tell from the garden," he says, and one of these tracks might ultimately mean less sculpture. Bob is considering letting vines cover some of his least-favorite pieces, and simply burying others in the ground. "That way, if I change my mind, I can dig them up again," he says with a laugh. "I'm bored with sculpture. More and more, I'm obsessed with plants, and using them as sculptural forms. I guess I'm jaded. I like things that change, and plants change."

In the end, gardening on this acre of the Oakland Hills is a form of play, with the garden as the playground. "From my first job, I got used to being able to play," Bob says. "Play is the absolute best thing, period. There's a

It has become something of a cliché to say a garden is made up of rooms, but in the case of Bob Clark and Raul Zumba's landscape, it is an unavoidable allusion. One example is the plush green living room carpet of the upper terrace, ABOVE RIGHT, where tulips, forced in refrigerated pots, will bloom on the steps; or the "wreck room," RIGHT, with its somewhat wrecked steel furniture suite. All that is left to do is sing the praises of this brilliant, adventurous garden, in chorus with a group of joyous, open-mouthed prickly pear cacti (**Opuntia** sp.), OPPOSITE.

whole group of people who have moved away from the garden as something serious and impressive, to making it something to be enjoyed, to be played with. I've been spoiled in a way, since I've had clients who've allowed me to do that. But really, I don't think I could stop myself if I tried."

The gardeners commissioned horticultural artist Archie Days to create a cacti and succulent garden, RIGHT, on a level spot beside the house. The result is barely believable. In one area, an assembly of glazed pottery statuette planters, set in terra-cotta pots planted with various echeveria, sempervivum (hen-and-chicks) and other rosette-forming succulents, worship a pipe and rusted metal totem. The object of their adoration is ringed in rebar and topped by a variegated century plant (*Agave americana* 'Medio-picta'). Members of the tribe include (left to right) green aeonium with leaves like giant rose petals; reddish blades of phormium; and a bushy shrub, *Dodonaea viscosa* 'Purpurea', above a leafy peren-nial, *Heuchera* 'Palace Purple'. At the base are two golden barrel cacti (*Echinocactus grusonii*). One might want to adopt the religion of cacti and succu-lents as manifested by these plantings. Another of Days's creations, ABOVE, is a living "stained-glass win-dow," with lines drawn in succulents on clay pots in a bed of red manufactured clay gravel, and ground-covering sedum—all topped by a Medusa hairdo of flowering echeveria and surrounded by lumpy organ-pipes of *Echinocereus maximiliana* cacti.

PART 3

GIVING BACK

A friend told me a story about his neighbor—a story that I've heard in various forms and countless times over the years. It seems that the neighbor, armed with chainsaw, pole pruner, and electric hedge clippers, spent the entire weekend pruning his trees. He shaped the red maples in front of the house into giant, top-heavy lollipops. He topped the row of young hemlocks that ran along one side of the property and sheared their branches on both sides until they looked more

like a chain-link fence than anything alive. More than his neighbor's noisy industriousness, what upset my friend was that he could see no reason for any of this activity. The trees weren't growing into any power lines, or obstructing any views, or crowding the driveway or walkways, or casting unwanted shade on any other plantings. Until they received their unfortunate "haircuts," they had actually been handsome, healthy specimens.

Whenever I hear such tales, I can't help but think that this man, and so many of us, act sometimes out of pure instinct. Like primitive cave dwellers imagining that ferocious predators lurk behind every bush, some people look around their yards and see only "enemies"—in insects and critters, in weeds, and even in trees they may have planted themselves but which have dared to thrive and grow. Even though nature ultimately turns out to be uncontrollable, there seems to be great satisfaction, for some, in fighting the never-ending battle.

Though this impulse to "tame the wilderness" may have evolved with *Homo sapiens* and be part of our genetic makeup, this doesn't mean that we need to continue to use and abuse the world around us. A large part of my work over the years has been to convince people that conquering nature, rather than being a birthright of the species, is instead actually threatening life as we know it. I extrapolate from my friend's neighbor to the millions like him around the world. Instead of mutilating a few trees, we see the burning down of rain forests to open up grazing land for cattle. Instead of dousing a backyard patch of weeds with herbicide, we see farmland drenched with hazardous chemicals. Meadow, swamp, and woodland are turned into shopping malls with hundreds of stores and acres of parking lots. A result of this mindset is that the natural world is treated not as a natural wonder, but as a resource, to be exploited in the name of profit and progress until it is mined out, exhausted, ugly, and stripped of life. The motivation behind it all—what feeds this frenzy—is that everyone in the world wants to live the way Americans live, and Americans most of all.

Bruce Grimes and Geoff Kaiser are giving back by weeding and encouraging natives on their property, PRECEDING SPREAD, LEFT, such as the rare pink *Silene pensylvanica*, RIGHT. ABOVE: One of the greatest losses of habitat occurred in the United States as much of the tall grass prairie was plowed up for farmland. OPPOSITE: Although overharvesting vegetation contributes to modern ecological problems, at least farmland is alive—preferable to asphalt-paved parking lots—contributing oxygen to the atmosphere and allowing water to seep into the earth.

Scientific evidence warns us that the world's species are on the verge of a catastrophic mass extinction, the sixth such event according to the fossil record. The current trends that scientists say are leading us down this path include the introduction and the spread of invasive species, pollution and global warming, over-harvesting products from the land, loss of habitat, and isolation or "islandization"—plant and animal communities fragmented by development. The last time such a mass extinction occurred, 65 million years ago, most experts agree that it was caused by a meteor or asteroid hitting the earth, the dust from the explosion causing a dramatic climate change that led to the death of many plants and all the giant dinosaurs.

This time, we humans are the asteroid.

Some people argue that the very success of humans in consuming the earth is natural, and if it does lead to species demise, this is just nature taking its course. I would like to think that it doesn't have to be an all-or-nothing proposition, that we can learn to both consume less and replenish more, to live more in balance with the cycles of the natural world. As gardeners, we are more in tune with these cycles than others, and in a unique position to do things that might counter the destructive forward momentum of this "asteroid." I propose that all of us adopt a horticultural version of the Golden Rule, doing unto nature in a way that honors all that nature has done for us. We should give back something for everything we receive, and strive to make our small corners of the world more hospitable to lives other than our own. We should share these ideas with friends, teach them to our children.

What we do in our gardens may seem inconsequential in the grand scheme of things, but none of us lives in a vacuum. What we grow, how we treat the land, our attitude toward the natural world: all of this affects our own ability— and that of our neighbors—to enjoy the type of world that we want for ourselves and those who follow. Treating nature with respect and reverence—helping it thrive and spreading its bounty rather than aiding in its destruction—is clearly a spiritual notion. As a garden lover, view it as part of your responsibility to the beloved.

ACT NATURALLY

Charity begins at home, and there are many ways we can help the earth as we work in our gardens. One of the most important things is to adopt organic gardening practices, using natural fertilizers and pest controls instead of their chemical counterparts. Making and using compost is integral to organic methods, and it may also be one of the simplest ways we can give back to the land. There are many "recipes" for what some gardeners call "black gold," as well as various commercially made bins and tumblers, all of which ensure that enough heat is created to kill any weed seeds or soil pathogens the pile may contain. My compost is all made in open piles where I layer vegetable matter, twigs (to keep some air in the pile), and a nitrogen source (such as horse manure or grass clippings). When one pile gets about waist-high, I move to another and by the time the third pile is under way, I may be able to use some of the product from the first.

Compost works more slowly than chemical fertilizers, having much lower levels of nutrients. But its benefits go far beyond giving plants a quick chemical fix. It helps build up the soil, both lightening heavy soils or beefing up sandy soils, in both cases helping keep the proper amount of water in the root zone.

Integrated Pest Management (also called IPM) focuses on natural controls, including the introduction of beneficial insects, and recommends use of pesticides only as a last resort, and then only those with the smallest negative impact—oil and soap sprays, for instance. Using poisonous chemicals to control insects, weeds, and fungal diseases can be overkill, literally. We wouldn't try to destroy an ant's nest with a stick of dynamite, because of what might occur: windows in the house blown out, underground utility lines ruptured, a huge crater in the front lawn. But many people don't realize, or choose to conveniently ignore, that the effects of chemicals often go far beyond the targeted problem, to include "collateral damage" that might not be so obvious. A careless application of herbicide, on a patch of weeds under a tree, might be the reason the tree itself is suffering. Many insecticides attack pests but will also work their "instant kill" on the beneficial insects that eat those pests. Birds and fish and other higher forms of life are also not immune. About 5 billion pounds of pesticides are used annually throughout the world, and by some estimates these chemicals kill 67 million birds a year. Even if pesticides don't directly kill birds, they cause harm by killing off their food supply. Neil Diboll, the owner of Prairie Nursery in Westfield, Wisconsin, likes to ask his lecture audiences, "Do you like birds?" After giving everyone a chance to smile and nod their heads, Neil adds the punch line: "Then you had better get used to bugs."

Tolerating insect damage as part of the cycle of life in the garden can be

One of the best ways to give back is to recycle vegetable matter into compost. Fresh material goes into the first compartment of Barbara Robinson's compost bins, ABOVE, ages in the middle section, and is finally taken, fully decomposed, from the third bin. OPPOSITE, BELOW: As one saying in defense of nature's creatures goes: "Do you like birds? Then you had better get used to bugs." An insect chewed a hole in a canna before the leaf unfurled, creating this pattern. OPPOSITE, ABOVE: I took it as a possible sign of long-term climate change when I found a crocus geometer, or cranberry looper, further south and east than usual: on the screen door at my New Jersey home.

looked at as part of a new relaxed garden aesthetic, one that is healthier for the land and less of a strain on our backs and our pocketbooks. "Perfect" can sometimes be accomplished "naturally," with a lot of hard work. But in the garden, perfection is more often unnatural, a miracle of chemistry that requires regular applications of fertilizers and pesticides. This is especially true of the perfect lawn. Lawns posted with "Danger" flags are not just a threat to those who walk on them: lawn chemicals and fertilizers, which easily run off during rainstorms into streams or ponds, or seep into groundwater supplies, constitute a major source of water pollution in some areas.

Letting go of the pastoral ideal of a perfect greensward could, in the end, be liberating. In this time-hungry world, you'll have more time for other activities—perhaps to tend more satisfying areas of the garden, or turn the compost pile. Being satisfied with a green patch of whatever happens to be growing in your area—the new definition of lawn for the new century—also means that you will no longer have to worry about poisoning your kids as they romp around, barefoot in the grass.

Water quality always ranks high on the list of concerns of Americans. But we have to add a concern about quantity these days, as demand outpaces nature's supply. When I travel around the country, sometimes it's hard to tell where I am without looking at my plane ticket. Especially in the naturally arid southwestern and western states, wealthy communities have gardens that look pretty much alike. Their trick? Just add water, and you, too, can have an English garden, or a golf course, in the middle of a desert. Wouldn't it be a whole lot more interesting, not to mention prettier, to have a cactus garden in the desert? The result of such profligate water use is that even the mighty Colorado River peters to a trickle and then disappears before reaching its natural destination, the Gulf of Baja—its entire

James David covered a galvanized stock tank with a cedar trellis, transforming it into a beautiful outdoor cistern, OPPOSITE. Thousands of gallons of rainwater, which would otherwise be lost, are collected in this jumbo container and then trickle through the garden.

flow sucked out by municipal and agricultural water users, many of them hundreds of miles away.

In areas with more annual rainfall, we tend to take water for granted, thinking of it as endlessly renewable and self-cleaning through the evaporation-precipitation cycle. The predictability of the weather is one of the reasons I chose to live in the Northeast. In the old days, my part of New Jersey received nearly an inch of rain a week, fairly regularly throughout the year. That much rain makes woodland, and woodland is what I love. But five years of drought in the past six (including the worst dry spell in recorded history) have reminded me how uncontrollable the weather is, and forced me to look differently at my consumption of water.

Where I live people rely on underground wells which, in the 1980s, were dug to a depth of around 100 feet. My well is dug to 300 feet, and 500 feet is not uncommon. During one of the recent droughts, homeowners had to have old wells dug deeper to get any water. In a town nearby, many homeowners saw their wells go dry when a neighboring golf course dug a deeper, larger well, and now these residents have their water supplied by the golf course operator.

Ever since I saw James David's beautiful cistern in Austin, Texas—a galvanized stock tank from a farm supply store, gussied up with a covering of cedar lattice—I've wanted to have one of my own. Mine is much smaller—a 55-gallon drum elevated on a wooden stand—which I initially hooked up to 300 feet of soaker hose installed in my nascent woodland garden, to help the plants off to a good start. I would fill the tank once a week and let the water ooze out through the hose. I didn't want to use sprinklers that water from above, since a great deal of water is lost through evaporation. Plants also tend to be knocked down by the force and weight of the water, which means more staking for me.

Once the plants in the woodland were established and could get by with what nature provided, I moved the drum to the house, where it now collects water from one of the downspouts. The drum fills and overflows quickly, and I need more storage to make this a viable watering system, especially since we get the rain when we don't need the stored water. Commercially made drums can be expensive, but the potential is there: if you collected water from a rooftop area of 1,000 square feet, you would have 625 gallons for every inch of rain.

Getting the woodland garden to be drought resistant didn't happen overnight. There was no soil on this site, and the medium I imported was nearly 100 percent compost, so I used a water-retentive polymer gel (available at most garden centers and nurseries) in every planting hole. When wet, these coarse crystals (which somewhat resemble kosher salt) swell up to many times their original size, and then slowly release the water back into the soil. It's important to follow the directions, and not use too much dry crystal in a hole, or else, when it rains, your soil (as mine did) may erupt like Vesuvius with clear cubes of swollen gel. Now I wet the crystals before adding them to my planting medium, which also assures that water reaches the plant roots in those important days right after planting. Manufacturers claim that the safe, biodegradable gel should last up to three years, but in my Zone 6 garden it seems to disappear after a year. This product seemed to help, although usefulness varies, according to other gardeners.

Besides holding water in the ground by adding compost and other good things to the soil, mulching is very important, especially on new plantings. When you read instructions on mulching that say, for example, to add three inches of mulch to newly planted perennials, you may wonder, as I do, where room for all that stuff is supposed to be. Keeping in mind that the mulch should never touch the stem or trunk of any plant makes the task even harder. I use this trick: when installing many perennials or small shrubs in a location, I turn the empty pots over each young plant. After spreading the mulch, loosely and thinly, I carefully remove the pots, leaving a circle of clear area around the plants' crowns.

The type of mulch is up to you, but consider the source and the aesthetics. Avoid any mulching product that contains weed-suppressing chemicals. Big mulch chunks never look good, and can easily float away in heavy rain. Avoid using "green" mulch, such as live wood fresh from the tree surgeon's chipper. The fresher the mulch, the longer it will draw nitrogen away from plants, as microorganisms use that element to break down the material. Gravel or crushed stone can work as a mulch in the right place (such as a gravel garden). My favorite mulch (and to my eye, the nicest looking) is one that is often free: chopped leaves. Oak leaves are the best, since they curl and will not become waterlogged or compact.

Someday, hydrogen may provide the energy to run everything, and the waste product is water, but until then, we can't afford to make the stuff. As gardeners whose creations rely on water, we can take the lead in helping conserve this vital resource.

WHAT IS UGLY?

A miracle happened in Michigan in the late 1990s, when pretty became ugly. Purple loosestrife (*Lythrum salicaria*), a lovely flowering perennial which is also an insidious invasive plant, came to be looked upon as ugly for the damage it causes. Plants like purple loosestrife are considered "botanical pollution" for a simple reason: only one plant can grow in one place at one time. As invasive plants spread, they supplant natives which might have been the food or home of some other organism, which in turn might have contributed to something else higher on the food chain—a chain that leads to the top, to us. Purple loosestrife is a good example not just because it is so visible, but for what it does to the wetlands it conquers. Besides self-sowing wildly, it establishes thick, woody roots that quickly begin drying up the area around them, lowering the water table while raising the soil level. As of 2001, loosestrife had invaded wetlands in all of the lower forty-eight states except Florida. Many states have enacted laws that ban the sale of loosestrife plants or seeds.

Invasive purple loosestrife is native to Europe and is believed to have come to North America as seed stowaways on ships or as a colonial medicinal plant. I don't use the word "invasive" for indigenous plants that simply colonize their local community. Just about all aggressive indigenous plants have a reason for being. For example, poison ivy (*Rhus toxicodendron*) is often considered a scourge at the seashore, but this opportunistic plant, which quickly moves onto disturbed land, can help to hold dunes and fight erosion. We may be the only species allergic to the vine. In fact, the berries of poison ivy rank among the highest of all woody plants for food value to wildlife.

Many problem plants come from other places, and are referred to as "exotics." If you look at a plowed field in spring, you will see many exotic weeds germinating. You won't see local plants, because they are warm-season species, adapted to sprout when the weather is settled and air and soil temperature are

I do not find blooming purple loosestrife pretty, ABOVE. On the contrary, the plant's vigor makes me a little queasy. What's wrong with loosestrife? For one thing, it runs rampant in wetlands, where it raises the soil level and lowers the water table, effectively drying up the ground and changing the habitat. Another problem: only one plant can grow in one place at one time, so wherever *Lythrum salicaria* is on the loose, native plants can't keep a foothold. The food chain is interrupted, as animals that fed on the missing plant—and may in turn have been food for something else—disappear from the area. This chain ultimately can lead to humans. OPPOSITE: In woodland, vine weeds such as English ivy (*Hedera helix*), myrtle (*Vinca minor*), oriental bittersweet (*Celastrus orbiculatus*), and honeysuckle (*Lonicera* sp.) choke the forest floor and climb the trees, changing the ecosystem.

warm. By the time the local plants germinate, the exotics are established, casting shade and competing all too well for moisture and nutrients. One way to fight these pests is with fire. When permits can be obtained, Chicago-area landscape designer Cliff Miller (whose work is profiled in this section) does "controlled burns" in late spring to destroy seedlings of cold-season exotics in his native prairie restorations.

Purple loosestrife is not a problem in its native habitat because insects that eat the plants act as natural checks there. However, the impulse to introduce the purple loosestrife eaters to North America is questionable. In various studies these predators have been shown to greatly reduce loosestrife populations, but once they eat all the loosestrife in an area, will they turn to other plants? More studies need to be done, but introducing the insects here just might prove to be the most promising method to control loosestrife.

Unfortunately, loosestrife is only one of many invasive plants. Its reputation is now greatly tarnished, but gardeners and nurseries are reluctant to give up on many of the others. English ivy (*Hedera helix*), which isn't killed by most over-the-counter herbicides, has invaded woodlands—blanketing the ground and climbing into the crowns of trees—in nearly every place it has been planted. (When I saw ivy inundating Thomas Jefferson's Virginia estate, Monticello, I couldn't help thinking that it was Britain's revenge for losing its most valuable colony.) Two other popular groundcovers, *Vinca minor* (also called periwinkle, or myrtle) and the Asian *Pachysandra terminalis*, also readily escape from home plantings to smother acres of woodlands. Yet all three of these plants are still commercially available and planted by many landscaping professionals. One garden designer I know always speaks with glee about fast and easy plants that "spread," which is a flattering adjective to him but a warning sign to me. This man might not be so cavalier if he was installing these spreaders in his own garden instead of those of his clients.

Many nurseries not only sell potentially invasive weeds (which have the great advantage of being easy to propagate), but tout them and, in some cases, build a business

around them. Several nurseries deal almost exclusively in crown vetch (*Coronilla varia*), a deep-rooted, quickly spreading plant with a ready market, as many state highway departments use it to control roadside erosion. Unfortunately, seeds from crown vetch spread far from the original plantings, and once established it is tough to get rid of. As much as we think government intrudes too often into our lives, it will apparently take the federal banning of sales of certain plants to get the industry, unwilling to police itself, to alter its point of view.

Some people have told me that some of my ideas, especially my abhorrence for invasive plants, smack of horticultural McCarthyism. What's wrong, they ask, with an aggressive plant in the artificial context of a garden? I admit that not everything can be drawn in black and white: a plant that spreads widely in a warm climate might be killed in a colder one. But when nursery owners ask how they can possibly determine which new plants will become problems without putting them in quarantine beds (or gardens) for twenty years,

Most native American perennials are warm-season plants that germinate in late spring. By then, cold-season European field weeds, such as mustard and its relatives, have sprouted and crowded out natives. Plants that love disturbed sites include colorful cresses in a meadow north of San Francisco, ABOVE. In this area, eucalyptus trees have replaced many native trees, and scotch broom (*Cytisus scoparius*) has pushed out plants that used to grow in the nooks and crannies of the hillsides. OPPOSITE: Queen Anne's lace (*Daucus carota*) is another such weed, with a long taproot. Unfortunately, it is sold in seed mixes for "wildflower" meadows. In time, a meadow that at first is only sprinkled with this plant will be dominated by it.

I might offer a few insights. If a non-native shrub has berries that birds feast on, watch out. If it colonizes vast areas in its natural habitat by wildly self-sowing (as many grasses do) or by sending underground rhizomes many feet a year (like most bamboos), be suspicious. If it is a vine that leaps over trees, be assured that it will jump the garden fence, as well.

Gardeners should also be aware of these traits and keep an eye on any plants that exhibit them. The last thing we want to do is bring a new, untried beauty into our gardens and find ourselves fighting it for the rest of our lives. If you aren't sure how a new plant behaves, don't risk the chance of creating a "passalong pest" by giving seeds or divisions to gardening friends. If a plant does become a problem, consider eliminating it before you become too attached to it, and then warning others.

Every gardener has examples of this, and one of mine is a *Ranunculus* variety named 'Buttered Popcorn'. A catalog from a West Coast nursery warned of the plant's aggressive tendencies, but suggested that in cold climates it would probably not be a problem. One fall a fellow gardener encouraged me to plant a single four-inch pot of this beauty. Cold didn't seem to deter it: even in my Zone 6 garden, it was off and running from the start, growing through most of the winter. By springtime it had spread so far and wide that I had to begin ripping it out. Whether I liked the pretty cream and pale green leaves or not, I knew one thing for sure: I did not like spending my precious gardening time digging out a problem that I had inadvertently caused. Broken bits seemed to sprout leaves overnight, and it took three years of careful hand weeding to eradicate the offender. In the process I lost several choice plants that the *Ranunculus* had overrun, giving new meaning to the phrase "companion plantings." In 2001 I saw hundreds of pots of this plant at my local Wal-Mart, ready to seduce a whole new wave of gardening suckers.

A woman I met is thrilled that her Queen Anne's lace, originally from a canned meadow mix, comes back every year in bigger swaths. But now the plant is popping up in a park across the street. Another person controls his more vigorous plants by removing three-quarters of each colony every spring. But what if he moves away or dies? No one will be there to control these plants; or if the new owner digs them up and puts them on the compost pile or sends them to the neighboring recycling center, they may escape.

To battle existing invasive plants, we might consider enlisting the aid of the same groups who clean litter from the roadsides. Local watershed conservation groups often attract scores of people to their annual creek cleanup days, and teaching such people how to identify and remove invasive exotics might help make a dent in their populations. Municipalities might be encouraged to set a good example by banning the planting of invasive trees and shrubs in public areas. We somehow need to educate our neighbors about this problem, as Pennsylvania gardener Bruce Grimes tries to do through his local newsletter, because as long as their properties harbor invasive plants we will be forever fending them off at our borders.

TO THE RESCUE

In the mid-1970s, Michigan resident Patty Shea became distressed by a story familiar to many of us —the ever-increasing pace of development and the resulting destruction of the woods around her home. Fighting to preserve the habitat of native plant populations should always be our first line of defense. But in the many cases where that isn't possible, plant rescue groups, such as the one Patty and a friend began in 1975, are a good last-ditch option.

That first year, Patty arranged for some of the wildflowers she rescued to be planted in the gardens at Cranbrook, a historic house in Bloomfield Hills, Michigan, and others were sold to benefit the property, netting a grand total of $67. From that modest start the program has grown to include nearly one hundred volunteers who rescue thousands of plants a year. The annual Cranbrook native plant sale attracts gardeners from all over the state, and in its best year the proceeds topped $30,000. In 1999, Patty moved to northern Michigan, where she has started a new rescue group to benefit a local land conservancy. (For a list of native-plant and land-preservation organizations, see page 244.)

While all the interlocking pieces of an ecosystem are destroyed by commercial and residential development, plant rescue efforts tend to focus on the most fragile of the flora—the native herbaceous plants, especially the spring ephemerals, which bloom and die back and are thus easily forgotten. "There are often people saving the trees," Patty says, "but people rarely think about saving what's under the trees. It always amazes me how

unfamiliar people are with our woodland natives. Rescuing them, and planting them in public places or selling them to the public with information on how to grow them, is a way to show people how beautiful they are. Seeing that, maybe they'll get interested in saving the habitat, too."

Patty suggests checking local laws before undertaking a plant rescue, especially those concerning the disturbance of native species. Rescuers must also first receive written permission from the owner of the property. Working with a local organization will help your credibility when approaching developers or landowners. In supporting Cranbrook, Patty's group has grown so in reputation that now they are being directed to sites to be developed by the developers themselves.

In Michigan, the plant rescue groups work from April until June and again in September and October, with some volunteers going out into the woods as many as six days a week. Part of the challenge, Patty says, is teaching volunteers how to recognize plants they may have never seen before, let alone in a near-dormant state. "Most books only show what plants look like in flower," she says. "Most things we rescue are not in flower, so it's a matter of teaching volunteers what the roots look like, what the emerging leaves look like. It's amazing how sharp their eyes become, how much they learn." The only downside, she says, is poison ivy. "Otherwise, it's a win-win proposition."

Patty Shea's passion is rescuing native plants (such as *Trillium cuneatum,* ABOVE) and teaching others to do the same. For thirty years her various plant-rescue groups have, with the owners' permission, dug plants from properties before the bulldozers arrived. The plants are then potted up and sold to raise money for other rescues, for conservation groups, and to develop a public wildflower garden. Some of these plants now thrive in Patty's own garden, OPPOSITE.

Pink *Geranium maculatum* and lavender *Phlox divaricata,* ABOVE, create a subtle analogous color combination. The slightest breeze ruffles the leaflets of the maidenhair fern, BELOW. Little white flowers, LEFT, dangle from the arching wands of Solomon's seal (*Polygonatum biflorum*).

Above the foliage of twinleaf (*Jeffersonia diphylla*) is the jewel in Patty Shea's garden, LEFT, the yellow lady-slipper orchid (***Cypripedium pubescens***). BELOW: American Jack-in-the-pulpit, allegedly one species (***Arisaema triphyllum***), often shows a variety of color from pale green to this eggplant-purple-striped individual. BELOW LEFT: The colorful woodland serves as a foreground to the antique-brick house.

REPARATIONS

I want to grow many plants, and many of them are not "local," a word I use as a further distinction from native or indigenous. "Native" has come to refer to a plant that originated in North America. "Indigenous" should mean that the plant comes from a specific region, but it is often used interchangeably with "native." "Local" means nearby, perhaps from within a fifty-mile radius of your home site. It's wrong to think that a plant is somehow better for your garden just because it is native to somewhere in North America. If a plant originated in California and you intend to grow it in Georgia, it is not necessarily better or more appropriate than something from Japan. If the plant from California turns out to be an invasive thug in its new southeastern digs, it would, in fact, be worse than any well-behaved Asian.

Although I admire Franklin Salasky for growing only local plants on his Long Island property, I could never devote my whole garden to that. I lust after too many plants, from all parts of the world, and this causes me some moral angst. As part of my Golden Rule philosophy, I have to make reparations for the privilege of practicing multiculturalism in my garden, and I've done this by setting aside an area that I call a "mitigation garden."

Of course, making healthy soil and a well-tended garden is a form of mitigation, but I'm suggesting that we go further, and try to grow as many local plants as we can, as development destroys their natural habitats. If we grow them well, we will at least be preserving their genes for the future—for a time when they may be needed in a restoration project. It may even be possible that some native plants—such as the Pacific Northwest yew (*Taxus brevifolia*), the source of the anti-cancer agent Taxol—may contain as yet undiscovered medicinal compounds.

We should also grow these plants because they are lovely. You might base your planting on the former wilderness that once lived where you do now. If you live in Arizona, you might make a desert garden or a dry alpine arrangement, using

There is no danger of a hosta takeover, which makes these Asian foliage plants, RIGHT, useful for lovers of native plants, since they will not escape the garden. Of course, hostas are not for dry Southwest gardens or in Northern California because they are consumed by the European snails that thrive happily there. But what is native? Native often means North American. I try to talk about *indigenous* (meaning plants from a region) and *local* (for plants from as little as a ten-mile radius of the chosen location). OPPOSITE: Cliff Miller developed the edge of a wooded site, removing alien weeds and replanting the species that once thrived in this eastern Illinois location. The edge is where the action is in every natural habitat: the edge of the ocean, the edge of the woodland. Edges are where plant communities meet, and they often contain a wide diversity of species. The edge planting here, shown in autumn, includes asters and goldenrod.

Scout the dog stands on the footbridge to the land off-island where I hope, someday, to grow plants that originated in a ten-mile radius of this site, RIGHT. Finding the plants is not a problem in this rich habitat, where mountains, rivers, flood plain, and woodland converge. The hard work is keeping the site free of alien weeds. As fast as I remove the exotic plants, others move in. After shrub honeysuckle and multiflora rose were removed, dormant seeds of the mustard relative dame's rocket (*Hesperis matronalis*) sprouted, OPPOSITE. Although this biennial is beautiful, it too will have to go as I bring the planting back to "natural." *Hesperis*, a biennial, is easy to remove, unlike the perennial purple loosestrife, which has thick woody roots that have to be dug out with a pry bar and spade.

all the elements found in those locations. Cliff Miller, the Illinois landscape designer, is hired to restore and re-create tall grass prairie communities. If these restorations are large enough, they can function much like their progenitors, and Cliff finds that animals, ones often thought to be long gone from an area, may return.

My mitigation garden is a half-acre that I call "little new jersey" (lower case intentional), in which I hope to be able to grow only plants from within a ten-mile radius. My part of the world, along the edge of the Appalachian Mountain range, is historically rich in flora, so I will have many species from which to choose, if I can find them.

Discovering what grew in an area since the last Ice Age can be challenging but not impossible. Surveys of flora in preserves and state and national parks are available. Books on woody plants, herbaceous species, and wildflowers often include the plants' original range. Online sources can also be found. Many botanical gardens also have regional flora displays, living "catalogs" of the plants that once lived in a particular place.

The "mitigation garden" in New Jersey will be the hardest of all my plantings to make and maintain. The invasive weeds move in to the disturbed land as fast as I remove them. Progress is slow, but progress, nonetheless.

STEWARDSHIP

Progress can mean progressive approaches to necessary development, but unfortunately, it is too often a synonym for greed. To most people, progress means *more:* more manufacturing, more high-density housing, more outlet malls and box stores, more traffic jams, more pollution. "Intelligent development" may seem like an oxymoron in many localities, but it is something we should always be fighting for. We need to care for what is as well as what might be, for what is under our feet as well as what is beyond the stars. It may seem hard to have patience for people who work to erase the landscape, but we need to try. The first step is to discover what we have in common: our connectedness, not just as fellow human beings, but as part of the web of life on which our survival depends. Those of us with more awareness need to teach our neighbors that humans are not above or apart from the world but an integral part of it, with great power to do either great harm or great good. If we fail to change our views and continue on our present path, we will end up like the amateur arborist, sitting up high in the tree and blithely sawing off the branch on which he sits. Soon, that branch, the world, will come crashing down around us.

There is so little "wilderness" left. In some places animals and plants have managed to return to a semblance of what they used to be. Although those near-wild places should be considered sacred and kept intact, we all know they are not. In this country, parks and preserves can be "declassified" and opened up to logging and mineral development at the whim of a new administration. We lament the loss of the rain forests of Central and South America, and decry the industrial development in China, but such losses are everywhere. Just as developers gain support for their projects by appealing to self-interest—more jobs, lower taxes, increased GNP—those of us on the opposite side need to employ similar tactics. People who care little for loss of species when a rain forest is felled may be more concerned to learn that some of those species might have been sources for new medicines or foods. Preserving clean drinking water—or any water at all—is yet another reason to slow development. While some of us may be cynical about the political system, we still need to recognize its potential clout and support any candidate for any office, regardless of party, who demonstrates genuine regard for the environmental health of the land.

If we accept a place in the ecosystem and in the ecology before us in the garden, we come to understand the interdependence of every entity and how fragile this fabric is. "The Earth is part of my body," said a Nez Perce elder of the Pacific Northwest. "I belong to the land out of which I came. The Earth is my mother." Cliff Miller likes to paraphrase another Native American. "There's a quote from Chief Seattle," he says, "that goes something like 'How can you own the land? It's my grandfather's ashes.'" Cliff's abbreviation for this is "We are what we step on."

Donating time and money to organizations dedicated to preserving plant and animal species and their habitats is important for all of us. Becoming involved with such groups may help expand our awareness of problems and possible solutions. As Bruce Grimes and Geoffrey Kaiser become more

While visiting gardens in Australia I met a family who had planted native species and developed a buffer of greenery at the edge of their property, OPPOSITE. They convinced their neighbors to do the same, and together they created a flyway for birds and other animals being squeezed by the rampant development in that country. BELOW: Sensitive amphibians are indicators of the health of a garden and the planet, one of many reasons to provide refuges for these animals, and to urge municipal governments to do the same. involved in various botanical societies and local conservation groups, they have come to a greater appreciation for the native flora on their property, and have decided to bequeath the land to a conservancy that will preserve it as open space, never to be developed. Cliff Miller, besides working for private clients, helps neighborhoods and new housing developments discover alternatives to lawn-only landscapes, and volunteers his time and expertise to local conservation groups.

On a smaller scale, Barbara Elliot, who lives on a one-acre lot in a development in suburban Philadelphia, became an avid birder in midlife, and as a result she began to change the way she took care of her yard. She has created plantings of shrubs and flowers that the birds use for food and cover, and provided a small pond for water. She admits to being a gardening novice, and only has time to undertake a few small projects a year, but says her efforts have so far been well rewarded.

"On one weekend I counted thirty different kinds of birds in the yard," Barbara says. "I've seen many different butterflies. We have a frog that visits the pond each spring, and an Eastern American toad who laid thousands of eggs in it. I even enjoyed the two small snakes I saw last summer, which I take to be another sign that the environment is improving.

"There's still way too much lawn," she admits, "but little by little I will try to reclaim it to more natural plantings." Her "Backyard Wildlife Habitat #20975," as certified by the National Wildlife Federation, is still a work in progress. Thousands of gardeners across the country participate in this national project, and some of them band together with neighbors to make a good thing even better. By working together to link such stands of native plants from yard to yard, neighbors can create "flyways" and "greenbelts" that provide food and cover for birds and insects and ground animals. These green spaces provide safe highways for animals that breed in one place and migrate to feed and live in another.

Barbara now dreams of taking early retirement from her corporate job and somehow turning her passion for wildlife into a new career: teaching people that what they do in their own backyards can have much wider repercussions. "It seems simple to me, a no-brainer," she says, "but most people don't understand the ramifications of what they're doing." Saving the planet really means preserving life as we know it. With more teachers like Barbara, we just might manage to save the world, one corner of the backyard at a time.

BAMBI, PETER, RICKY AND CHUCK

Four-legged intruders are a universal problem for gardeners, and successfully protecting our plants from their predations can be a challenge. Urban gardeners may suffer from squirrels or cats digging up plantings. Raccoons plague other gardens in towns around the country. In parts of the South, alligators pose the problem. Coexisting with wildlife becomes more and more of a problem as development leads to shrinking habitat. The concentrations of animal populations along with the elimination of natural predators have led to a serious dilemma. Most of us want to live and let live, but it is hard to have our gardens and not have them eaten, as well.

Gardeners who live in deer country, which includes many of us in the United States, know what havoc these critters can wreak on home plantings. Now we are also seeing the price of this overpopulation on wilder parts of our environment. In the precious few undeveloped sites left, overbrowsing by deer has destroyed much of the understory. Along with the eaten wildflowers, seedlings and saplings are gone, which means, as older trees and shrubs die, there will be no young ones to take their places.

There are several camps, the Bambi lovers, the Bambi haters, and perhaps, the hunters in between. The idea of shooting deer sounds terrible, but after

It is easy to see damage when it happens. Dealing with a problem is much harder. Welcoming "nice" animals while keeping out "nasty" ones is especially challenging. We are concentrating animal habitats and have destroyed most natural predators, but the animals that eat our gardens are often ones that do very well in suburban, and even urban settings, such as the deer that ate this hosta, ABOVE. Sherran Blair fenced the rear of her Ohio property, OPPOSITE, to stop the four-legged hosta-lovers.

seeing a few communities where deer have been corralled into public parks in which they starve to death in the winter, I begin to side with the hunters. Then I see beer cans tossed by the side of the road during the deer season, and animals injured by bungled marksmanship, and I drift to the other side.

Some municipalities have tried to protect their parks by hiring professional marksmen to cull the deer herds under strictly controlled conditions. But such efforts have aroused virulent opposition of animal rights groups, and in populated areas such hunts, no matter how well supervised, may pose a danger to human life as well. In one community I visited, hired bow hunters killed seven deer in one week, while forty-five were killed that week in car accidents.

If you think that an answer lies in deer-proof plants, think again. With few exceptions, most of the plants touted as deer-resistant will be eaten when the food supply dwindles. There is hope for gardeners, however. Nearly every deer repellent on the market works, as do similar home brews. The question is how long they work, and how often they need to be applied. Some have to be reapplied after each rainstorm. Repellents with polymer additives help them stick to the plants for a longer time. Some of the preparations have potentially dangerous chemical contents, and some smell bad to us, as well. Experts say that it helps to alternate repellents, to keep the deer from getting accustomed to any single kind. Read the labels, choose your weapon, and consider product warnings.

In New Jersey, I put up inexpensive plastic netting fence. The tough, black fence is eight feet high, and when it was first installed I hung white rags on it, which mimics the way white-tailed deer warn each other of danger—by raising their tails and showing the white undersides. The fence is barely visible, hidden by the trees around the boundary of the property. I am lucky that the river closes off some of the entrances to the garden; if not, I would have to add more fencing and install cattle grating at the entrance to the parking area.

Deer will rarely walk on an unsure surface and, unless pursued, will not jump without a clear space to land. I visited a garden in Ohio that was decimated by deer, except for the vegetable patch. This space had only the protection of a two-foot-high fence, but the key was the raised bed inside the fence. The deer didn't have an open space to land between the sides of the raised beds and the very low fence, so they didn't jump. Betsy Clebsch, a *Salvia* expert who lives north of San Francisco, protects her garden from deer with two four-foot fences about five feet apart, between which she grows her roses.

Many of the animals that populate the suburbs today do very well around people. Opportunists such as raccoons, bears, squirrels, rabbits, and woodchucks will take the path of least resistance—to our garbage cans or vegetable gardens—for their next meal. The most successful way I've seen to protect vegetable gardens from these critters is with metal mesh fencing—"chicken wire." A two-foot tall fence with another foot buried underground will keep rabbits from jumping over or tunneling underneath. A similar but taller fence, with a strand of electrified wire across the top, often works to deter climbing critters such as raccoons and woodchucks.

I've also tried repellents to keep animals besides deer out of my garden. Mothballs helped keep digging animals from getting to my freshly planted bulbs and also helped with the problem of rodents that crawl through the snow to strip the bark around young trees, which kills them. I place a few mothballs at the base of the trees in autumn, and try to keep mulch from touching the trunks, as this gives the critters an easy way to tunnel up to the tree's base. Dryer fabric-softener sheets kept squirrels from digging in my woodland garden, but their odor kept me from digging in it as well.

FRINGE BENEFITS

The fringes of the ten-acre Field estate, north of Chicago, could have been planted in lawn, as are most places in the neighborhood. But the owners—sensitive to plant communities that thrived on their site years ago—opted to have P. Clifford Miller, a Lake Forest, Illinois, landscape designer, restore and expand the remnant prairie on the property. Today, this two-acre area does contain a lot of grass, but some of it is five feet tall or more, and it sways and dips with the shearing winds blowing across Lake Michigan to the east and the savannah flatland to the west. Among the steel-blue blades of the big bluestem (*Andropogon gerardii*), flowers of forbs (non-grass herbaceous plants) add sprinkles of pink, orange, yellow, and red, a spectral display that reaches its crescendo in autumn, when the grass blossoms turn tan and gold.

Cliff Miller is one of the country's pioneers in tall grass prairie restoration, having worked on such projects since 1980. "Back then it was uncharted territory," he recalls. "It was difficult to get the plants. The only oaks available were ones you shouldn't be planting here, and the same with maples. I was buying and digging trees from farmers, from construction sites. There wasn't a lot of information, but since I was one of many people getting into this at the time, new information was being generated daily."

Many of the early restoration attempts failed, but something new was learned with each one. These days, seeds and plants for such projects are far easier to find, with some seed companies and nurseries specializing in

Cliff has always had a passion for nature, starting with childhood explorations of a vacant lot beside his parents' house. His first forays into gardening were with terrariums. "As a kid I loved amphibians and reptiles, and I would catch them and build miniature environments for these creatures to live in, little rivers and little oak groves." In a way, he has simply expanded that focus in his current work, in which he helps restore or preserve full-scale environments for the plants and animals he loves.

Cliff began doing landscaping work in high school and college, mostly rehabilitating existing plantings. After college he landed a position as naturalist with the Lake County Forest District, teaching schoolkids about the environment. In the process, he deepened his knowledge of the local plants and animals and the natural communities in which they lived—in particular, the prairie, the woodland, and the savannah. He later held a series of jobs with contractors and landscapers; finally he set up his own business in 1984. But in many ways, he still considers himself a teacher.

"It's a social obligation for me to teach people what they've got just outside their doors, and how cool it is," he says. "It's one of the main reasons I'm still living in this area. I'm not a very social guy, and I was planning to go and live in the woods, on forty acres I'd bought up north right after college. But I made a decision to come down here and teach people about the wonders of nature, instead of being upset about what they were doing to it."

The Field estate is one of many projects Cliff has worked on over the years. The spaces around the house are formal, and planted in a traditional estate landscape style,

these species. The years of hands-on work done by Cliff and many others has increased the base of knowledge to the point that a careful restoration practitioner can now be relatively sure of success.

Instead of having acres of lawn, the owners had P. Clifford Miller, a Chicago-area landscape designer, re-create what might have been on the site in the years before development, PRECEDING PAGES. Determining what "might have been" was easy, as a remnant tall-grass prairie still exists at the rear of the property. Cliff was originally brought in to manage this area, but he encouraged the residents to expand it and turn much more of the lawn into grass-prairie and colorful forbs (non-grass herbaceous perennials) that look wonderful in the autumn. Part of the landscape remains formal, as can be seen reflected in the pond, ABOVE, but from farther away, the decidedly informal landscape is evident, OPPOSITE.

with lawn, specimen trees, and small ponds. Originally he was brought in to conduct a managed burn of the remnant prairie at the back of the property, but the owners gradually came to value Cliff's input regarding many decisions about the estate. Though he was formally trained in neither ecology nor design, Cliff is a rare hybrid—a horticultural professional who has broad knowledge of the natural world often missing in the résumé of landscape architects, as well as spatial sense that most scientifically based restoration experts lack.

One phase of the work at the Field estate was to redesign the area connecting the prairie remnant with the two ponds (originally designed by the late landscape architect Ralph Synnestvedt). These ponds were rebuilt, expanded, and replanted in a more naturalistic style by Cliff and landscape architect Peter Cummins. This area now serves as a bridge between the natural and formal parts of the estate.

Over the years Cliff managed to nearly triple the size of the property's prairie, by removing secondary growth (including about one hundred weed trees) and expanding the habitat back into that cleared area, but it is now about as big as it can get. "It's a formal estate," Cliff notes, "so you don't want prairie up to the door. These prairie remnants are basically gardens. Maybe they are doing a little bit for ecological diversity. You might have

Beautiful pink boltonia blooms late summer to fall by the edge of the pond that divides the formal landscape from the informal tall-grass savannah planting. The bridge is another remnant of the landscape's earlier development. The pond makes the two styles appear logical together, and the bridge softens the aesthetic and physical transition between the controlled and wilder plantings.

a few things, maybe a few rare butterflies or things like that, but there are no bison roaming around. They aren't big enough to sustain real prairie wildlife. But it's an emotional thing: people like to feel that they are doing their piece. And if one person does their piece and another person does another piece and another and another, maybe you eventually get three hundred acres connected, and maybe those three hundred acres will have a real impact."

Cliff often warns potential customers that re-creating even a small prairie remnant is not a simple, one-time job. "There are a lot of prairies that are lawns again because people weren't told how to maintain them," he says. Newly planted prairies need management for at least the first few years. Depending on whether they were planted from plugs or seed, they may need to be mowed. Cliff sometimes spot-sprays problematic weeds (such as white leaf clover and Canada thistle) with herbicide. Even the cover crops used to keep weeds down until the prairie plants become established, such as perennial rye and red fescue, can become a problem.

"You can't just throw a can of seeds over your shoulder and walk away," he warns. "It's foolish to think we're going to be able to re-create what took ten thousand years to evolve and have it establish itself just like that. Only after there's been a long-term establishment of a knitted plant community do you get into a low-maintenance, light-a-match kind of thing. In the early years, everything is so dynamic it takes a lot of work."

Cliff has donated his time, managing land and doing controlled burns for conservation organizations, supporting this with income from more conventional landscape design projects. "It's not profitable, but it's a commitment I made to myself and the natural world, that we would always keep that relationship. I'm part of the world, and I like to feel connected to it." Cliff's favorite time of day to meditate on this connectedness is "the crepuscular hour"—the time either just after sunset or just before sunrise when the light becomes magical and many species of wildlife are most active. He created a miniature prairie and wetland in a secluded corner of his backyard, and he will sit quietly as the stars come out, watching and listening to the wildlife come and go.

"I was out walking my dog the other day and I just had to get down and look up at the big bluestem," he says. "I'll occasionally walk into the middle of a wetland, get eye-level with the water, and see what's up." Flopped on his belly in the swamp, trying to decipher the secrets of the natural world, Cliff is reenacting his childhood, when he spent hours on the floor of his bedroom, staring through the glass at the worlds in his terrariums.

"I'm still a big kid, which is one of my problems," he admits. "My wife calls it lack of maturity. I call it curiosity."

Cliff Miller is a "hybrid" of a landscape designer, able to work both on constrained landscapes and those that appear unrestricted. In truth, it is a hard task to develop a functioning simulated plant community, such as the prairie restorations that are Cliff's specialty. Once established, however, the maintenance costs are much less than those for the watering, spraying, and mowing of a grass lawn. Of course, such a natural landscape is also much more hospitable for wildlife and arguably, humans as well. Just imagine this bridge before, when the land around it was planted in short, mown lawn. Not only does it look better now, but the air around it is filled with the music of birdsong, the hum of bumblebees, and the fluttering of butterflies.

PATHS

I've often said that the shortest distance between two points is the front walk. That's how the mail gets from the street to the slot in the front door. But when utility is not the only intent, as in the case of the garden, a path can take on greater purpose. Generally, a path has a single destination, but it can also take you to things along the way. Geoffrey Kaiser and Bruce Grimes walk their twenty-two acres every day—to take in the views, check on various projects in progress, visit the pawpaw patch, and for countless other reasons. But a path can also be its own reward—a trip to enjoy in itself.

A path can be made simply to walk along while meditating, thinking, ruminating on the events of the day. For this kind of path, a smooth surface is probably best, as a path with varying grades, steps, or obstacles might be more of a distraction than a meditation. Sometimes a simple worn path of hard-packed dirt is adequate. Often mowed lawn makes a pleasant path. Cliff Miller's paths through tall grass prairie appear to be grass lawn, but it is simply mowed prairie. The plants that grow tall on either side of the path are the same as the ones turned into turf through cropping. Cliff has augmented these weaving green walkways, however, by

The easiest way to produce a path in a meadow or prairie planting is simply to mow one; most plants in these landscapes will appear much like lawn when mowed and will hold up as well to foot traffic. Cliff Miller provided such a mown path for his Chicago-area clients, ABOVE, allowing them to stroll through the tall-grass prairie and see flowers, birds, and insects close up. When landscapes are made to re-create, restore, or renovate what once was wild, we have to discover new ways to get into them. Clearly, driving a golf cart across a mown lawn won't work. Most of the paths in the woodland garden of Bruce Grimes and Geoffrey Kaiser, OPPOSITE, are narrow tracks wide enough for only a single person, but in a few places, wider paths have been made by weeding or seasonal mowing between trees.

planting special plants beside the path or in places where they turn or converge. There, giant grasses may flank either side of the path, shooting up like fountains or curtains that must be parted to pass.

Mowed paths are fine, but a path can be made of nearly anything. Crazy paving (a blend of materials, such as brick, tile, ceramic shards, stone, or gravel) can be wonderful, and in a small garden, may be a feature in itself. In tiny quarters, watching the ground could produce a more complicated experience, making the garden seem larger than it actually is.

If mobility is the point, the paths should be smooth—but that doesn't mean they have to be extra wide or paved in asphalt. In my New Jersey garden, there are a few obvious paths, but hidden behind the main crescent-shaped border is a wider utility path that provides the quickest way to get the cart to the compost pile.

Perhaps a path is one part of a garden where form really does follow function. Consider whether the function is efficient utility, like the mail delivery, or to visit a fragrant plant, or maybe sit on a bench for a spell. In that case, the path might lead "nowhere"—you come to that place, stop and enjoy the experience, turn around and come back, better off for having ended up at this particular "dead end."

NATIVE SONS

A wrought-iron garden bench, large enough for two, balances on a rock ledge overlooking the lower part of the property of Bruce Grimes and Geoffrey Kaiser. Behind the bench, the moss-covered ledge is home to a variety of indigenous plants, including partridgeberry, several native azaleas, mountain laurel, and *Corydalis sempervirens*. Mature trees—hemlocks, pines, oaks, and tulip poplars—tower overhead, while below, a narrow spring-fed creek winds through a steep, green glen. Dotting this landscape are boulders, some as large as small houses, their sides crusted with moss and lichens and their tops home to colonies of ferns and wildflowers.

This scene seems so natural, so right, that it's easy to be fooled into thinking that all these two men have done is clear some paths to make the property accessible. But a closer look reveals evidence of human intervention: hybrid rhododendrons growing among the natives, primroses lining one of the paths, and wire cages protecting some of the young woody plants from the depredations of deer. The most telling evidence is the list of plants that are missing from these twenty-two acres: Japanese honeysuckle, multiflora rose, and most of the other invasive species that infest all the neighboring woods.

While everything here seems to be as it should be, little of it would actually be this way without serious, long-term intervention. All the chores common to gardens everywhere happen here: propagating, planting, weeding, pruning, moving and removing plants; building walls, paths, bridges, a water garden, a meadow. But for Bruce and Geof-frey, working in these woods goes beyond simply gardening. This is their sanctuary, the place where they both learned and practice their eclectic faith—an amalgam of Quaker, Jewish, and Native American beliefs. As they have re-formed and repaired this piece of eastern Pennsylvania for nearly thirty years, the land, in return, has helped give shape and meaning to their lives.

After building a log kit house overlooking the glen, they set about trying to restore the overgrown property, to reveal and highlight the natural features they had fallen in love with at first sight. Under the canopy of mature trees, too many smaller trees com-peted for light, and a tangled understory thicket rose fifteen feet high in places. Unlike many gardens, where there is a blank slate (maybe a former farm field) upon which the gardener's desires can more easily be imposed on the land, the massive process of editing a garden out of this woodland took Bruce and Geoffrey years.

They had no plan to follow; their ideas, Geoffrey says, simply unfolded over time. "A flat property would have been easy to lay out on paper, but with the steepness of this site, and with the underbrush so high, it was really hard to draw anything up." They began by working outward from the house, cutting pri-

A typical outcropping on this property, its rocks lit by the set-ting sun, PRECEDING PAGES, would not be visible without dogged control of exotic weeds. What looks like a place just left on its own is more like an arch-aeological dig, in which layers of time have been peeled away to reveal what was once, and in this case, always there. OPPOSITE: One of the older gardens in this book is this place that was developed—yes, developed—by Bruce Grimes and Geoffrey Kaiser. Could the house be seen from the deep ravine if the weeds had not been removed through the years?

marily witch hazel, spicebush, and several *Viburnum* species, all of which were abundant and so tall they obscured any views. As they cut, they searched for other species that they wanted to preserve and nurture, among them the mountain laurel, dogwood, and redbud that now abound on the property. They also discovered some surprises, including a grove of native pinxterbloom azaleas (*Rhododen-dron periclymenoides*), which provides an example of how one gardening partner can temper the extremes of the other, to the ulti-mate benefit of the garden. The plants had been stunted by browsing deer, and Geoffrey didn't care for them at all. "I originally thought they looked like dumb honeysuckle bushes that dropped their flowers after a day," he admits, and if Bruce hadn't liked the plants so much, Geoffrey might have let the deer keep on nibbling. Instead, he coddled the plants back into health, and they are now a spring highlight, covering about an acre of woods near the house and blooming in a subtle range of colors from white to pink to lavender.

Geoffrey had grown to love *Viburnum prunifolium* as a child, while similarly "garden-ing" a patch of woods on his parents' nearby property, but Bruce didn't share this senti-mental attachment for this shrub. He called it "stinkbush," for the bad odor given off by the wood when it was cut, and at his insistence, they hacked most of it down. "I didn't know what it was, and since I didn't have a name for it, I didn't respect it," Bruce recalls. "Then I learned the name, and that it had food value for wildlife, and we allowed the plants to grow back."

After thinning the overgrown understory, the next step was to thin out the canopy. In 1977 they brought in a forester who marked

two hundred trees for removal. "We sent him to six acres in the far corner of the property," Bruce recalled. "That way, if we didn't like the result we never had to go back there again." Fortunately, besides providing many cords of firewood and the lumber used to frame their barn, they liked the leaner look of the thinned-out woods. Over the next several years they brought the forester back two more times, to

When a rare indigenous plant is discovered on the property, the men take action. The ripening fruit of the twin-leaf (*Jeffersonia diphylla*), ABOVE, is held on a stem above the leaves. When ripe, the urn-shaped capsule splits and the seeds are instantly dispersed. The germination rate is not high, but human intervention—harvesting the capsules a few days before they naturally split, and carefully placing the seeds in the duff around the parent or in a similar location nearby—improves success and enlarges the colony. OPPOSITE: When all is well, a spectacular native may appear, or one purchased from a native plant society can be encouraged to grow and multiply, as in the case of the yellow lady-slipper orchid.

mark two other six-acre sections. All told, they removed about one thousand trees.

In nature, a few individual trees will slowly grow to shade or outcompete their neighbors, which eventually die. Thinning accelerated this natural process, speeding up the growth of the trees left behind and propelling the whole woods toward a more mature feeling. "The property had grown up like a carrot patch since it was last logged in 1915," Geoffrey says, "and like a carrot patch, if you leave all the seedlings you never get any decent carrots—they all come up crowded and stunted." He has also removed the lower limbs from most of the larger trees. This allows more light to reach the understory plants, and opens up long, inviting vistas through the woods that add to the feeling of maturity.

Bruce continues to thin the woods selectively, cutting some trees for firewood and "girdling" others by sawing a deep circle

around the trunk near the ground, which stops the flow of nutrients between the roots and the crown. These dying trees are left standing to provide food and habitat for wildlife. "At every stage, as a tree rots, there are different animals and insects that live in them and feed on them," Bruce says. They also nurture a number of tree seedlings, some of which will become the next generation of forest as the older trees die: "in-case" trees, Geoffrey calls them.

Trees were also removed from two other parts of the property, each about three acres, which became Bruce's dry meadow and Geoffrey's marshy meadow—the latter area watered by the outflow of a pond they dug in a low spot by the creek. Skunk cabbage (*Symplocarpus foetidus*) quickly spread throughout the marshy area, and later muskrats made a home in it, too—critters that Geoffrey could live without, since they eat the water lilies he grows in the pond. "Geoffrey made a perfect habitat for the muskrats, so they moved right in!" says Bruce with an unsympathetic laugh.

In wetlands, America's answer to the hosta is native skunk cabbage (*Symplocarpus foetidus*), which creates its own perfect picture, OPPOSITE. The stream that flows through the property feeds a circular man-made pond, ABOVE RIGHT, which overflows into a less-contained pool, and finally into cleared wet areas where the skunk cabbage now grows. After heavy rains, the small stream can swell to a roaring torrent. RIGHT: Geoffrey Kaiser designed and built two bridges across the stream, including this one. PRECEDING PAGES: One of the most spectacular scenes on the property is when the native pinxterbloom azaleas (*Rhododendron periclymenoides*) flower in the springtime (LEFT). The shrubs appeared as deer-gnawed stubs in the understory until enough trees had been cleared to allow the sunlight in. Seeds of the native wild columbine (*Aquilegia canadensis*) germinated in this hospitable spot in the leaf litter on top of a rock (RIGHT), and have been producing an ever-more stunning show each year.

The self-trained botanist of the pair, Bruce has inventoried five hundred species of plants on the property. They have introduced about a hundred of these, while the rest were there when they bought the land, and are mostly trees, shrubs, flowers, ferns, and grasses native to the area. One rare find was the large tway-blade orchid (*Liparis liliifolia*). Bruce fell in

With spaces opened and competing plants removed, the natives returned, such as the single, blooming mayapple (*Podophyllum peltatum*), and young Jack-in-the-pulpits (*Arisaema triphyllum*), OPPOSITE. In developing their 22 acres, Bruce and Geoffrey began close to the house. Early on, paths and steps, ABOVE, were built that penetrated ever deeper into the undergrowth, and non-native rhododendrons were planted. Today areas around the house are maintained as places for "garden plants," such as primroses and peonies.

love with this dainty beauty, prompting Geoffrey, the gardener of the pair, to try to make more. Propagating them by division over several years, he ultimately turned the original four plants into a colony of twenty-seven. He has practiced this multiplication trick with a number of the native plants on the property, sometimes working by division, other times scattering fresh seed in various places, including in the leaf mold on top of the boulders.

Geoffrey also built a footpath to the rock where the orchid grew, one of many paths of various sizes that meander around the property, all of them leading to some viewpoint or favorite plant or feature they like to see. The widest, at eight feet, runs the length of the property and allows access for a tractor to bring logs out of the woods. Intermediate paths, such as the mown path that winds through the meadow, are about four feet wide, while most are only single-file tracks, just wide enough for one foot to be placed after another. Each path creates a different feeling, Geoffrey says. "I especially like the sense of release when I'm leading a group of visitors down one of the single-file paths and it comes out into the open, and we can relax and talk about where we've been. It feels like when the clouds part for the sunshine."

In the steepest spots Geoffrey builds stone steps that seem to have been in place forever. He achieves this look by carefully placing all the stones with their grain aligned and their weathered sides up—"green side upside, brown side downside," as Bruce puts it. Geoffrey uses similar methods when he builds dry stone walls, or rearranges the smaller boulders to open up a new path or close off one he no longer wants used. One circular walled area, where the men host a local Native American affinity group for drumming and other cere-

monies, looks as if it could have been built hundreds of years ago, by the Lenape Indians themselves. It is one of the many examples of the subtle artistry—and artifice—of this place, where all that looks natural is not necessarily so.

But Geoffrey's hand in the garden is not always so subtle. Bruce is a proponent of native plants, and would plant nothing else if it was solely up to him. Geoffrey, unfortunately, has fallen for various exotic species over the years. For example, he loves gaudy hybrid rhododendrons, and planted thirty-five of them on the hillside near the house before Bruce convinced him that the native members of this genus also had merit. He planted red and yellow primroses along one of the paths, and has an obsession with common snowdrops. Great sweeps of them can be found in late winter in various places on the property. In one area by the pond, where almost a dozen native herbaceous species appeared once the shrubby overgrowth in the area had been removed, Geoffrey had an unfortunate inspiration one day and planted yet another sweep of snowdrops. "They disappear by the time any of these other plants come up," he says, a bit defensively, and Bruce can only throw up his hands and laugh.

Besides promoting the native species on the property, Bruce has taken on the Sisyphean task of trying to rid the twenty-two acres of exotic invasive weeds. "When we opened up the woods I realized we might exacerbate the weed problem, so I promised myself I'd keep after them," Bruce says. He uses no herbicides in this effort, instead spending hours removing them by hand. He deals with stilt grass (*Microstegium vimineum*), which springs up in any disturbed ground, by cutting it down with a Weedwhacker before it goes to seed. One plant of garlic mustard (*Alliaria officinalis*), a relatively recent arrival on the property, may produce hundreds of seedlings the following year. In his search-and-destroy mission against the mustard, he not only weeds his own property, but part of the adjoining land, too.

Weeding the woods is one of the ways that Bruce is trying to restore the land to the way it was when it was *Lenapehoking*—a place of the Lenape. He knows that, ultimately, he won't be able to keep the woods clear of weeds by himself, and has been trying to enlist others in this effort through articles in *Turtle Talk*, the neighborhood newsletter he edits. "I want to believe that people would care more if they knew and understood the problems our natural landscapes are facing, and if they cared, they would be motivated to act," he says. "But like Jonah going to Nineveh, I don't think people are listening."

Over the years Bruce and Geoffrey have learned much about plants and animals and how to create a garden that includes both. But sometimes they find this knowledge a mixed blessing. "If all this greenery was just 'bush' we could live here in blissful ignorance," says Bruce. Adds Geoffrey, "We've climbed the Tree of Botanical Knowledge and learned to love and learned to hate. So we have to deal with our hatred of things like multiflora rose. That's why Sabbath is important, to set aside our hatred. I think every gardener needs to have a Sabbath, a break. "

Sabbath for Geoffrey and Bruce, as in the Jewish tradition, runs from sundown Friday to sundown Saturday. "It doesn't have to be that day, or even a whole day," Bruce says. "Even if you can just set aside one hour a week, where you get into a rhythm of doing things differently, it can be a help." On their Sabbath, Bruce and Geoffrey do no work in the garden, and if they talk about it at all, it is only to remind themselves of what they've accomplished. "One of the challenges of Sabbath," Geoffrey says, "is that Bruce is not to see the weeds." And sometimes, this actually works. But other times, as they walk through the woods on their day of rest, both men are busy making mental lists of things to do during the following days, and weeks, and years.

The daily walks they take through the property sometimes lead Bruce and Geoffrey to the wrought-iron bench on the rock ledge, overlooking the glen. Some days they pause there, sit side by side in the silence, listening to noises of the animals, watching the wind as it dances from tree to tree. Bruce might play an improvised tune on his recorder-like Native American flute, the haunting music giving voice to the spirits of those who once lived here.

From the bench Geoffrey looks out over the valley and sees a forest where everything is struggling for the light. "When I look from the cliffside I'm aware of my smallness in the scheme of things, as life keeps barreling forward. Some people worry about the demise of the human race. I think the earth would breathe a sigh of relief without us."

They watch the world unfold as the sun fades, the woods begin to grow dark. "We like to sit here at the end of the day," Geoffrey says, "and sort of disappear into the trees."

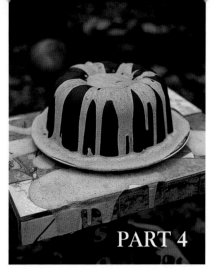

PART 4

GARDEN ESTEEM

Gardeners might just be the world's greatest apologists. "If only you could have been here a week ago," we say, sometimes adding the corollary in the next breath: "If only you could see this in two weeks." In some cases, the garden might really be in between seasons, or have been the victim of extreme weather, or be in a state of reconstruction. But often, excuses are an indirect appeal for reassurance, a way to get visitors to contradict our negativity and tell us how wonderful the

garden looks. Only if this gambit fails, and someone blithely agrees with our assessment, do we dare to go on the offensive and point out all the things that are right about the garden today, as well as the wonderful things coming three days, a week, a month, five years down the road.

When I visit John Beirne's wonderful New Jersey garden, I am met by a continuous stream of disclaimers. He tells me as much about what isn't there, or what is going to happen, as he does about the great things happening right before my eyes. Afterwards, I feel confused about the performance. Had I walked in on Act II and missed the overture, or did I leave before the finale? It's always a relief when my film comes back from the lab, and I can see the garden for the "first time," again, and enjoy all of John's plans and schemes.

When I called Evelyn Adams, a nonagenarian Massachusetts gardener, to ask if the *Trillium* were ready to photograph, she modestly confessed, "You're too late." I went anyway, and "too late" turned out to be breathtaking.

Evelyn isn't wrong to apologize, and neither is John, nor are any of us. Like doting parents, we would prefer that our gardens always be seen at their best, though (as with our chil-

What is acceptable as garden art is in the eye of the maker, if not the beholder, and many gardeners are taking greater risks. PRECEDING PAGES, John Greenlee and the artist known as Simple created a planting "bed" of living grasses in a gazebo with a roof of the 'Mermaid' rose (LEFT). Someone left the cake out in the rain (RIGHT); it was Ricky Boscarino, who used a bundt pan to make this whimsical garden ornament. OPPOSITE: Gardeners are great apologists. If only there had been more rain, we say, or less. When I called Evelyn Adams about coming to see her *Trillium* garden in Massachusetts, she told me I would be too late. I made the trip anyway, and what I found seemed the peak moment to me.

dren) we know this isn't always possible. Any gardener knows what might have been, what was, and what will be. Every garden does have its perfect moment, or series of moments; unfortunately, these are offered primarily to the garden maker, who has the privilege and opportunity—the luck —to be in the right place at the right time. In any case, these moments rarely seem to coincide with the arrival of visitors, and having one of them pass (sometimes helped along by foul weather) the day before a tour is only slightly less disappointing than missing it altogether. Dare to go away on vacation during gardening season, and on your return a neighbor might say something like "Your poppies were just gorgeous," meaning it as a compliment but making your heart sink. Peak moments are fleeting and easy to miss if we let ourselves get distracted by cares outside the garden. This is one of many reasons why, if I had the option, I would never leave my garden. I want to be here to see it all.

TAKING RISKS

How we view our gardens is important, because we are artists and, like it or not, many of us wear our creations, like our hearts, on our sleeves. When I was in college and later living in New York, my friends and I would talk about "making art" as casually as someone might say "making dinner." The process was important, and we didn't worry so much about the result —but then teachers, and later, editors, began to judge our work against their notions of what was "right" or saleable. We also reached a stage in our lives where making a living became a necessity, where this freedom—to experiment, to fail—became an unaffordable luxury for an artist with bills to pay. I look back on those days with some longing, because I would love to reconnect the lightheartedness of the process with the richness of the result, to feel free to make art in the garden and somehow silence the voices that whisper "Not that way!" at every unexplored fork in the path. This insecurity is compounded because, while some people make their gardens only for themselves, most of us need our work to be seen and, we hope, appreciated. Many good things come from having visitors in our gardens. Their feedback is one of the ways we can learn about new techniques, new plants, and new ways of seeing. There is the pleasure derived from giving pleasure, from sharing our plants and our passion with like-minded people.

But we take a risk when we open our gardens to the probing eyes of others. It puts our skills and taste on the line. Sure, a garden may never be done, but we care about what people think of it, every step of the way. It may help us to know that the gamble of exposing ourselves is an integral part of the creative process, a consequence of moving beyond the known into the new, and that nothing can be gained without taking such risks. If you stick your neck out, you might get your head chopped off; but if you don't stick it out, you'll never get ahead.

Every year, John Beirne tries something new and risks making some fantastic fumble—not in the eyes of those who visit his tiny garden, but in his own eyes. John didn't see Chanticleer—an estate garden in Wayne, Pennsylvania, that is now open to the public—until the summer of 2001. But he is a kindred soul to Chanticleer's director, Chris Woods, and his talented staff. Often I hear people say, "Oh, those lavish gardens shown in books, what do they have to do with me?" Chanticleer offers many good ideas that gardeners working on any scale can take home and try, and also exhibits a bold willingness to experiment with new plants and new schemes instead of repeating the same things (often the same mistakes) year after year. John has a full-time job, and has to share the home site with his father, who has his own vision of what a backyard should be. But he takes the same kind of risks on his fraction of an acre as Chanticleer does on thirty-one acres, with a massive budget and supportive board of directors. (Both Beirne's garden and Chanticleer are profiled in this section.)

One spring I phoned John to learn his garden plans for the coming year, and he informed me that he was "going blue." Hearing this from a man who is madly in love with the hot colors of the tropics was like hearing that he had decided to enter a monastery. I imagined the pale azures and mauves of English gardens, with spires of cold-climate delphiniums and *Meconopsis*. Beirne, born-again blue?

When I visited the garden later that year, I was surprised (and relieved) to see something far more outrageous: royal-blue Styrofoam disks taped to the barn-red garage wall, blue balls on sticks rising from his pots of tender perennials. Did it work for me? Not exactly. But as part of a longer process, it did work for John, because he saw how it could be made better the next time. And if he hadn't done it lightheartedly, with Styrofoam and spray paint, he wouldn't have been as happy to throw it out and try again.

I often wish I could be bold enough to sacrifice an entire season to such an exploration, but I have to admit that I'm chicken. Though I know a lot about photographing gardens and growing plants, when I get beyond dreaming of something artistic and actually set forth to do it, I can become paralyzed by negativity, telling myself, "It won't be any good" . . . "No one's going to like it" . . . "Why bother?" My insecurity tends to be inversely proportional to the size of the project. Planning and planting a garden can be a big production, with a cast of thousands of plants, so people can overlook the weeds, the flaws, for all the flash and buzz. It involves a different level of personal revelation than making a piece of garden sculpture, for example. Such things draw more attention, and, because of their uniqueness, are more subject to judgment and, perhaps, failure. But as with individual plants, the "failure" of a piece of garden art may simply be a matter of location. Like a plant, it can be tried out in different places around the garden until you find one where it works.

When I see the work of someone I admire, like Marcia Donahue, whose sculpture can be seen at Chanticleer, I get turned on, but also a little threatened. I worry about being original, since the best art is always original, and I dwell, perhaps a little too much, on being "tasteful," as if anything I do could ever please the whole world. I value my friends' wide range of tastes, some far different from my own, and they all have strong opinions. I'm sure Marcia would encourage me to loosen up, be more carefree in my garden constructions.

My friend Petie Buck is a talented garden designer with impeccable taste. She tends to be even more conservative than I am, but I admit to taking more than a little delight in seeing her nose wrinkle. I wonder what Petie would think of Marcia's Berkeley, California, garden. Full of sculptural plants and stone carvings, ceramic bamboo, with bowling balls and silverware used as groundcover and blue bottles stuck on branches, it puts a good number of noses out of joint.

The overall design of Marcia's garden is hard to see at once, since she has built and planted so much on her small city lot, and this could be where Petie and I part paths. While Petie might want to consider the garden from a bird's-eye view, trying to find a vantage point from which to see the overall plan, I would be reveling among the plants, enjoying a slug's-eye view of an *Arisaema* in bloom.

Marcia reveals a garden to me from another place, just as Petie does. Through Marcia I connect with the pieces, through Petie I consider the whole, but both of these women would say the same thing to me in the end: "Come on, Ken, stop and smell the roses, will you?" Petie might see in the roses a possible motif for a flower border, or a stencil border for the dining room. Marcia would probably delight in the rose's thorns and remark on how they might be used to decorate oneself in a pattern of ritualistic pierces and scars. Either way, making art is a way of life for both of them.

John Beirne manages to overcome, or at least co-exist, with his insecurities and create adventurous garden art. OPPOSITE: One year, "hazard blue" Styrofoam balls and discs had a tryout in his plantings. RIGHT: Sculptor Marcia Donahue merges work with play, art with humor. She can pre-visualize stunning moments, such as this combination of acacia with a similarly colored bowling ball.

OVERWINTERING
TENDER PLANTS

It might seem daunting to rescue tropical and subtropical plants from plantings outdoors in cold climates, before a killing frost will reduce them to mush, and then carry them over as roots in the basement or as cuttings on the windowsill until spring. But years ago, northern gardeners routinely dug *Canna* rhizomes and *Dahlia* tubers for storage. Of course, root cellars to put them in were once ubiquitous. It also seemed that in the days before central heating, cuttings of these plants rested happily on windowsills in suspended animation.

Although many of these so-called "tender perennials" can be purchased each spring at nurseries, it still makes sense to save them from year to year, and not just to avoid waste or save money. Changing horticultural fashion means that your favorite this year may be supplanted by a similar plant in a different color next spring. By carrying plants over, you can also have more of the plants you need, and in the case of tubers and rhizomes, bigger specimens with more flowers than you could get from the small plants usually available on the market.

The plants with tubers and fleshy roots are easiest to deal with. The general idea is to store these in a cool dry place. If the atmosphere is too wet, the tubers will rot; too dry, and they will shrivel; too cold, they might freeze; too warm, they will sprout too early and die. Just think of potatoes.

If the cool place—a basement, for example—is too dry, store the rhizomes and tubers in barely

moist sand, peat moss, or a similar material. If it is too moist, wrap the swollen stems loosely in newspaper. Ultimately, the biggest problem may be finding homes in the spring for all the excess tubers you end up with.

With herbaceous plants such as frost-tender salvias, coleus, or begonias, don't dig the plants from the garden, but take cuttings in September. Only two or three should suffice. Once rooted, they can be grown on a sunny windowsill, under fluorescent lights, or in a greenhouse. Pinch the growing plants once or twice so that they become bushy, and take cuttings from these plants in late winter to repopulate the garden in spring.

John Beirne improvises. He digs his cannas, elephant's ears, and dahlias once the killing frost has turned their foliage black, sometimes as late as Thanksgiving in his Zone 6b garden. The clumps are carried to a large piece of cardboard laid on the driveway and most of the soil is shaken off their swollen underground stems. He cuts the foliage and stems back to four-inch stumps and packs each variety in a labeled plastic bag, with plenty of dry leaves, and a few holes for air circulation. He stores

Growing tender plants—those that would be killed by frost in cold climate—is familiar to all of us who grow houseplants. Summering these plants outdoors is simple. Only when cold weather comes and we have to bring them indoors do we realize how huge some plants can become, like these bananas, ABOVE. Tender plants used directly in garden beds can be overwintered by taking cuttings to root and plant the following spring, for example, with *Salvia* 'San Ysidro Moon', OPPOSITE.

them in an area of the cellar that is cold but does not freeze, and leaves them until the following spring, when he is ready to plant them again.

Large potted specimens, such as *Ficus benjamina* 'Variegata' and *Euphorbia cotinifolia*, are pruned back hard and given reduced water and light (to induce a state of semidormancy), then stored in a dark corner of his bedroom. For plants from which he takes cuttings, such as coleus, he puts a few small stems—only three or four leaf nodes long—in moist perlite, covers them with a plastic bag, and sets them in a bright spot but out of direct sunlight. Once they root, he plants them in a humus-based potting soil in small plastic pots, and places them in a bright window or under fluorescent grow lights. To prevent them from putting on too much growth, he keeps the plants cool, and the soil is allowed to dry almost completely between waterings. In March he often takes new cuttings from these rooted plants, to make more for the garden.

The plants are sprayed with water every other day, which has little effect on humidity but discourages some insects, such as spider mites, and dislodges others, such as aphids, before they can get a foothold. If an insect infestation starts getting out of hand and a more serious spritzing is called for, John admits that he is not above sharing a shower with a *Ficus* or two.

Coleus, perhaps the most familiar tender foliage perennial, can be carried over indoors by taking cuttings, TOP. Giant

herbs, such as the dwarf banana cultivar known as blood banana (***Musa acuminata*** 'Zebrina'), ABOVE, can become houseplants in winter. Dahlias are tuberous-rooted plants originally from Central America. Popular with hybridizers, the variety of flower forms available today is nearly unimaginable—around 30 species and close to 20,000 cultivars. Some blossoms are as large as dinner plates; others are less than an inch across, such as maroon 'Stoneleigh Cherry', LEFT. Compact modern dahlia selections, FAR LEFT, do not need staking and produce many flowers. In cold climates, dahlia tubers must be dug up and stored.

Unlike the canna plants of the past, which had a narrow range of intense flower colors, foliage of these rhizomatous frost-tender perennials now garners more attention than the blossoms. BELOW LEFT: *Canna* 'Pink Sunburst' is a dwarf variety from Plant Delights Nursery. The striated foliage is exquisite, and the two-foot plants also bear flowers of a warm peachy-pink. Deep maroon foliage is an attraction of many canna varieties, some of which have pleasant flowers, too. LEFT: C. 'Constitution' adds baby pink flowers for a perfect combination. C. 'Pretoria', BELOW, has yellow-striped green leaves, as does C. 'Striata'. The former has orange flowers, the latter yellow blossoms. Canna rhizomes are harvested and stored like dahlia tubers. The modified stems of both plants can be divided in the spring.

IN GOOD TASTE

Recently, inspired by friends like John and Marcia, I decided to make a sculpture for my garden. The materials were experimental: cement and lightweight "aggregates" including nylon fiber, chicken wire, and steel wool. Dipping a conservative toe into the wild world of garden art, I thought I might make a representational bust of the garden demigod Pan.

Almost as soon as I began making my Pan, I lost any sense of objectivity. I chose to live with my discomfort and proceed, postponing the ultimate judgment for another day, and in this way the sculpture was eventually completed. Then came the problem of finding Pan a home. I first thought he might look best at the end of the stone bridge, or maybe in the garage, out of sight, but I forced myself to put him in the garden using a kind of tough-love psychology, telling myself not to be so afraid of what people might think.

I found a home for Pan I thought I could live with—on a wooden post in the gravel garden—and soon after, Tom Dolle came to visit. He is an arbiter of taste among my friends, and a few years earlier had compared the painted gate I made from an old iron headboard (page 25) to the hairdo of Marlo Thomas, star of the 1960s television series *That Girl*.

Tom looked at Pan, but didn't say a word.

Tom's ambivalence was my ambivalence: I, too, was reserving judgment. The important thing for me was to bear the weight of the waiting. I needed to let some time pass (and more than a day or a week) before deciding if Pan looked right where he was. It would have been a failure of nerve to have shoved my demigod into the gloom of the garage; but even worse would have been if I had never dared to make the sculpture at all. As it turned out, I eventually moved Pan to the place I had originally envisioned for him, and both he and I are happier for it.

My mother once used this mixed metaphor: "Sometimes you have to kick the bucket and live a little." Yes, I just might have to get over seeing this sculpture as a private revelation born of my deepest longings and insecurity, and try to get along with it. Someday—before kicking the bucket, I hope—I may discover what I think of Pan, or any other creation, regardless of anyone else's opinion. Art is in the eye of the beholder, and whether it comes to paintings on velvet or the Sistine Chapel or a homemade garden sculpture, there is one thing I've learned: I know what good taste is. Good taste is my taste, and yours. In the end, it is only our taste that matters and, given that, can we really go wrong?

My original plan was to nestle my sculpture of the demigod Pan in the shrubs across the path from the bottom of the arched stone bridge, but it migrated to a tall plinth made of a 6-foot 12-by-12-inch post. After a year there, I moved the bust back to the bridge, where it seems more at home and, although less obvious in the garden scheme, more effective. The sculpture is made of cement and nylon fibers spread over a Styrofoam wig form covered with chicken wire.

HOMEGROWN
GARDEN ART

These days, the only restriction on suitability for garden ornament might be weather resistance. From recycled plastic soda bottles to chiseled granite, it seems that anything goes.

Of course, filling the garden with ornament is not a new idea. Every self-respecting Roman patrician commissioned his share of two-ton bric-a-brac. Inspired by the Ancients, the British began filling their landscapes with classical ornament. Some of these were the real things, bought while taking in the sights on the Grand Tour of the Continent, but most were re-creations. Aristocrats went so far as to produce instant marble ruins recalling the Roman Forum. These somewhat frivolous garden shelters—aptly named "follies"—were built to punctuate rolling hills or set beside freshly dug lakes created during the Romantic Landscape movement of the eighteenth century.

It would be nice to have carved stone ruins and ancient sculpture popping up throughout your property, but that is quite unlikely. Nonetheless, every garden can include permanent ornaments. Carved stone may be beyond your reach, but modern concrete facsimiles are available in an unbelievable range of design and cost. You might even opt to carve or cast something yourself.

I tend to favor an informal, naturalistic style for my garden designs. But a naturalistic garden might look artificial with too many ornaments, or even

For centuries, designs for garden ornaments have strayed little from classical lines, such as original and re-created Greek and Roman structures, urns, and ornaments. But a different kind of line was drawn by garden artist Victor Nelson, who made a three-dimensional house in wire to hang in his garden, OPPOSITE. Chad Stogner of Vessels, in Decatur, Georgia, also eschews classical ornament. He has made casts of medieval building decorations, such as the gargoyle, ABOVE, from a fifteenth-century church in Roslyn, Scotland, but he is just as happy to cast and re-create picturesque sculptures from twentieth-century America.

one. On the other hand, in a formal garden it is harder to be casual, and placement of the perfect ornament takes on even more importance. In a tiny garden, it is hardest of all since every piece of the garden puzzle could be visible at once.

A decorative element might be bought or built before a garden is started and the setting made for it. This is most true when the item is selected in order to become a focal point: the termination of a vista, a point where paths intersect, or a place to rest along a path. In most cases, however, the decoration is brought in after the garden is made. I've often brought something to the garden thinking I know exactly where it will go only to find that it was not the best place. I carry the urn, sculpture, chair, what have you, around the place searching for just the right location. My Pan sculpture spent a year atop a post at the edge of the gravel garden before he found a better place. The sculpture now nestles in a green niche so that as you walk over the stone bridge, you are eye to eye with Pan. One nice thing about garden ornaments is that, while they may be set in stone (or concrete), they don't throw down roots, so they are more easily moved than most plants.

A wild combination of disparate elements converges in an ornamental pool, LEFT, by Atlanta garden designer David Bennett McMullin. Water is piped into an urn, planted with moisture-loving variegated yellow-flag iris (*Iris pseudacorus* 'Variegata'), that stands in the center of a galvanized stock tank. BELOW LEFT: Frank Sheekey painted found objects with a nautical allusion for his garden in Newport, Rhode Island. BELOW: In Logan, Ohio, a group of amateur and professional artists converge each summer to beat clay into garden art. The clay begins wet as extruded drainpipe sections. The artists create all manner of designs that are then fired by the pipe's manufacturer, and the artists' benefactors, Dick and Mary Holl.

The search for outdoor art can become a calling, as it is for the brilliant and charismatic artist Ricky Boscarino, who has created a pleasure ground he calls LUNA PARC around his home in northwest New Jersey, ABOVE. Ricky manages to assemble friends, LEFT, to help him realize his grander visions, such as the complete mosaic embellishment of the concrete wall in front of the house. BELOW: The artist Simple built twig fences and arches with John Greenlee for the latter's house and nursery in Southern California, but even working alone, a new garden artist should dig in. BELOW LEFT: For a few seasons, a simple blue-painted chair frame, retrieved from the trash, became a sophisticated sculpture in Ron Bentley and Sal LaRosa's garden in Bucks County, Pennsylvania.

PARADISE IN PROGRESS

There is an inviting porch on the north side of the main house at Chanticleer that lures visitors into its cool shade on hot summer days. Lush potted plants are clustered in the corners, and blue porcelain plates hang on the walls to either side of a fireplace. Dried flowers decorate the mantel, and in the middle of the porch a more ephemeral arrangement, changed each morning, features fresh flowers floating on water in a Chinese urn. A suite of upholstered wicker with thick cushions fills the room; a garden book lies open at the foot of a chaise, with more books stacked on the side table. It feels as if the owners of this former Main Line estate, fifteen miles outside Philadelphia, have stepped away for a moment, and you are distinguished guests awaiting their return.

The porch puts a new spin on the phrase "open to the public." It may seem traditional, but it is an unconventional space for a public garden, even one carved from a former estate, and hints at the other unexpected places to be found at Chanticleer. Just outside the porch it becomes obvious that the family is gone, along with any expectations of a soothing landscape. The calm has been detonated by horticulturists with a sense of daring and a sense of humor, who have created gardens that the wealthy family who once lived here might find as timid as a fireworks display.

Built in 1913 for the Rosengarten clan of chemical manufacturers, Chanticleer (named for the rooster in the fable "Reynard the Fox") began its transformation in 1990, and in the short time since it has become the most

exciting and, arguably, most innovative public garden in the United States. The quirky and flamboyant plantings on the thirty-four-acre property, combining all manner of brilliantly colored tender and hardy perennials, seem even more outstanding because they are made in the setting of a full-blown manor house and the shadow of mature trees.

It is unusual for a garden open to the public to welcome visitors as guests, but people who discover the porch at Chanticleer, ABOVE, can imagine they are the weekend company of the family that used to live in the estate's mansion. OPPOSITE: Nearby, a terraced lawn features a huge planted font that echoes the mansion's architectural style. In front of the planter is the wall of the swimming pool area, and behind it, a water feature, PRECEDING PAGES, which harkens back to Islamic designs and cools this spot as similar creations have done in other gardens for centuries.

Chris Woods, Chanticleer's executive director and chief horticulturist, is the impresario of this multistage production, and fortunate to have advantages beyond the dreams of most gardens. He has a staff of talented horticulturists and an operating budget large enough to develop and support the garden, as well as allowing him to commission works of art and hire outside consultants when necessary. Most important, the garden's directors are willing to take risks (such as when Chris suggested tearing down a house on the grounds to make a new garden space) that, at other institutions, would have been mulled over for years, if the ideas weren't tossed out of the boardroom at first glance.

Fortunately, Adolph G. Rosengarten Jr.'s will did not stipulate that the gardens at

Chanticleer be preserved as he had left them. Says one of Rosengarten's nephews, now a Chanticleer board member: "My uncle wanted to do a lot more than he did, but he was his own worst enemy. He never colored outside the lines."

"We're not restoring the Rosengartens' vision," Chris explains, "we're creating a new one." Chanticleer is billed as a "pleasure garden," and one of the goals seems to be to make every visitor feel as if everything—down to the exquisite floating blossoms on the porch—has been placed just so, just for their personal pleasure. "People talk about public gardens as living museums," says Woods, "but I like to consider Chanticleer as living theater. Here the staff are the actors, the stagehands, the makeup artists."

Part of this garden makeover has been to take typical estate garden elements and poke holes in them, letting the hot air out so visitors have room to breathe and relax, even laugh. Beautiful furniture (all made by the garden's staff) is placed around the property at strategic viewpoints, but some of the chairs are painted purple or chartreuse or decorated with leaf patterns or leopard spots. Near the porch two rocking chairs bask in the shade of an old silver linden, and from them a visitor has a magnificent view. Several bottles of bubble soap are at hand, ostensibly for the children, but Chris says he most often sees

Across the terrace from the porch at Chanticleer is a border, OPPOSITE, of yellow flowers and golden foliage. On top of the wall sits a shallow pot of gray-green echeveria and purple *Aeonium arboreum* 'Zwartkop'. ABOVE: A hidden walk between the terraced lawns leads to a planting of Marcia Donahue's sculpture labeled *Bambusa ceramica* 'Chanticleerensis', made of glazed clay culm sections threaded over steel rebar. Typical of its genus, this aggressive bamboo has burst its pot in its eagerness to escape into the garden.

adults waving the soapy wands and giggling as the bubbles drift down the hillside.

Besides the grand vistas, there are intimate spots with surprises just around the corner. Along the path leading from a terrace border of gold-leafed plants, a whimsical sculpture "grows." It is a rare clump-forming bamboo with an even rarer label—*Bambusa ceramica* 'Chanticleerensis'. Each of its multicolored ceramic culms, sculpted by Marcia Donahue, is topped by a rooster's comb.

One aspect of the garden that some find disconcerting is the lack of all but the most basic signs (such as "Restroom"). This is a philosophical and design decision that Woods carries all the way down to the level of individual plants, only a few of which are labeled. The lack of labels can be frustrating for plant lovers, because this plant-driven garden features many unusual species and varieties.

The view from the gatehouse driveway at the property's highest point overlooks former tennis courts that are now a perennial garden, PRECEDING PAGES, LEFT. The stone stairway leading down to this garden, RIGHT, has handrails that double as planters filled with rock garden varieties. The beds combine herbaceous plants, shrubs, tender perennials, and annuals in vivid colors, and feature a glider made by one of the garden's on-site artists beneath a rose-covered arbor. OPPOSITE: The maze, a nod to the estate's origins in agriculture, is planted annually in cereal crops, such as sorghum, corn, or wheat. In autumn, the colors of the grains enliven the landscape, BELOW.

Members of the eighteen-member garden staff can often be found at work, and most times they can answer any questions. But the lack of labels makes a visit to Chanticleer more an emotional than intellectual experience, by focusing visitors on the artistry of the place instead of the "signage."

"If I could find an aesthetic way to label our plants, I would, but most markers make gardens look like plant cemeteries," Woods says. Although he admits that much of the garden is "plant-driven," he reiterates, "We're not interested in being a botanical garden, or a collection-based garden. Some people have said that this means we're not primarily an educational garden, but, of course, I think we are. We're educating people in the art of horticulture, the culture of horticulture. The point of the garden is to show people the beauty of plants."

Chanticleer bears up to repeat visits, season to season and especially year to year. New plants are always being tried out, and beds receive regular makeovers. Entire new gardens are even being added. In 2001, Woods foresaw another decade of development before the garden and its staff settled into more of a routine: what he likes to call "the next thousand years of horticulture." The pleasure begins in the parking lot, where the planting beds are not simply maintained but gardened as assiduously as other areas of the property. Near the restrooms (worth a visit for their

elegant fixtures and beautiful flower arrangements) is a tropical courtyard, whose scheme changes from year to year but is most exquisite in late summer or fall, when its plantings of tender perennials reach their climax. This gem of a garden (tucked behind a house in which Adolph's sister Emily once lived, now the garden's administrative offices) has two levels, one paved and the other grassed, and depends primarily on foliage for its effects.

A four-square garden built on the site of an old tennis court has dazzling plant combinations that look good either from above, at the top of a granite staircase (complete with planted banister), or from a glider at garden level nestled in the shade of a vine- and rose-covered pergola. The terrace garden around the back side of Chanticleer, the estate's three-story main house, is as exquisitely maintained as the best gardens in England. More than one hundred container plantings, ranging from small pots only a few inches high to terra-cotta monsters a yard across, include any number of changing elements, including many beautiful succulents.

A vegetable garden, a cutting garden, and a grass garden occupy a sunny section of the property. A gravel garden ties an overlook point into the larger scheme of the place. From here visitors get the best view of a serpentine hillside planting made variously of wheat, crimson clover, blue oats, and sorghum, and of the three lushly planted naturalistic (but artificial) ponds. Below the ponds a collection of pitcher-plants (*Sarracenia* spp.) and other insect-eating plants live in a man-made bog; and on the perimeter of the property is a woodland garden, part of which features Asian plants nestling happily under a canopy of mature native trees.

Perhaps the most daring project at Chanti-

Three man-made ponds were dug at the base of the hillside below the ruin garden and the gravel garden overlooking the maze. These ponds, OPPOSITE, are elaborately planted with late-spring-flowering brown *Iris fulva*, purple *I. ensata*, big round *Allium giganteum*, and variegated sweet flag (*Acorus calamus* 'Variegatus'). The ponds can be viewed from an outdoor terrace built against a retaining wall cut into the hillside, ABOVE. Water that overflows the ponds forms a stream leading past shady woodland plantings.

cleer is a faux ruin of a house, its roofless stone walls visible above a copse of shrubs and trees. For many years Minder House, home to Adolph G. Rosengarten Jr. and family, stood on this site. But as the public garden developed around the empty house, Chris Woods came to see this unoccupied structure as a dead space at what he envisioned could be the focal point of the property. His first proposal was to make the house a ruin, but when it was determined that this could be done neither safely nor (more to the point) aesthetically, the board went along with the idea to raze the house to the ground and build a spanking-new "ruin." The structure, built on the footprint of the old house, was completed in 1999 and immediately became the property's much-discussed, somewhat enigmatic centerpiece.

Chris seems amused that people think the ruin is so risky, so new. He insists that it is "utterly traditional," completely in keeping with the Picturesque tradition in English landscape in the eighteenth and nineteenth centuries. This intellectual explanation aside, the fact remains that this gardening tradition is more than a century past, and the attempt to revisit it now is certainly a risk. Also remarkable is that a project of this scope and expense was even considered by a public garden, let alone carried to fruition.

An arched pergola for vines, such as passionflower (*Passiflora* 'Incense'), ABOVE RIGHT, leads to the garden that attracts the most attention at Chanticleer: the sheltered courtyard tended by horticulturist Dan Benarcik, OPPOSITE. Like many plantings in this pleasure garden, this so-called Tropical Teacup takes risks in its design, such as the year bromeliads were used as bedding plants, seen in the foreground next to a veil of horsetail and a red-leafed giant banana. RIGHT: Planted arches ornament the vegetable garden, where they advance down the wide central path.

Garden ruins are traditionally meant to bring certain images to mind, Chris says. But to mention those images, or relate the dreams that he says inspired various pieces of sculpture in the ruin, would (pardon the expression) ruin the chance that a visitor might bring a fresh point of view to the work. Too much art—too much of life, really—is over-explained these days, with more information given us than we ever need to know: where something came from, how and why it was done, the biography of who did it, and, worst of all, what we should feel and think about it.

Of course, this being Chanticleer, there are no signs at the ruin to give anything away. Indeed, it hardly looks "ruined" at all, with its neatly cut flagstone floor and the neatly mortared joints between the shiny, mica-laden stones in the walls. When asked how he plans to age the ruin, Chris gives this deadpan reply: "Wait three hundred years." But perhaps he might consider helping it along. Shotgun blasts might give the walls a few welcome blemishes and pockmarks, and weed trees could be planted in crevices at the top, as is commonly seen in those modern-day American ruins: abandoned houses in big cities.

One part of the ruin is worth revealing in detail, if only because it provides the clearest

The garden feature that inspires the most controversy at Chanticleer is the ruin, OPPOSITE. Director Chris Woods suggested partially tearing down an unused house at the center of the property, but it didn't turn out to be so simple. In the end, an entirely new structure—made to appear as a ruin—was built of mica-laden stone. The contrivance harkens back to the English landscape movement hundreds of years ago, when wealthy travelers discovered the ruins of ancient civilizations, which they re-created in their own gardens. Below the porch of the main house, visitors catch a first glimpse of the ruin, partially hidden behind shrubbery. ABOVE: Inside the ruin, a stone fountain features carved faces by Marcia Donahue.

contrast between what Chanticleer was and the challenging aesthetic experience it has become. In the smallest of the ruin's three "rooms" is a rectangular stone fountain, ornamented by six faces that Marcia Donahue carved out of mottled marble. Some are mounted above the water's surface, while others peer up from below. The fountain, on a timer, goes on and off without warning, and when the water is still, the faces resemble death masks; their thick lips seem bloated instead of voluptuous.

Whether you like the fountain or not, when the pump starts again and the water cascades from two sluiceways cut in the wall above, you have to take a little delight in seeing the faces come back to life. With their Mona Lisa smiles, the faces appear to be contentedly cavorting, and could be taken as emissaries for Chanticleer, beckoning to visitors: "Come in and play with us."

OPEN TO THE PUBLIC

Chris Woods and the staff at Chanticleer know what to expect by being open to the public. In many ways they have a certain sensitivity and empathy, having visited so many gardens themselves. One look at the restrooms, probably the most beautiful at any public garden, and you can tell that the public here is not seen as an unfortunate problem that must be tolerated, as it is in some gardens, but as a group of guests sharing a bit of paradise.

John Beirne has opened his home garden to friends and small groups by invitation. Now he has another garden, a horticultural therapy project made on a very public corner at Newbridge Services, the mental health agency where he works as a case manager. John started working in the garden with clients one spring. They helped prepare the beds, and then planted some of his fast-growing tropical plants, which made quite a splash for the gardeners and for the passing public by the end of the season. "To see the garden come quickly to fruition was tremendously satisfying for the group," John says. "I think it sends them a powerful message about efforts and results."

Visitors have already given John and his crew lots of positive feedback, which is the best part about having people come to your garden. But sometimes visitors can be trying. When we visit any garden, public or private, we have certain responsibilities to the garden maker, most of which boil down to a simple matter of respect. We should be careful about what we say, what we do, and even

Some gardens are exposed to scrutiny, either by invitation or because they are public; others are simply in plain view. People who come to Chanticleer are welcomed through the exquisite entry garden, ABOVE, which hints at the varied plantings that lie ahead. OPPOSITE: The gardens made by John Beirne and the participants in his horticultural therapy program are open to the public because they are located on a busy street corner. In both cases, the makers appreciate the kindness of strangers.

what we wear. It isn't polite to wear brightly colored clothes that draw more attention than the plants in the garden. Never peer into the windows of a house, and don't take photographs without first asking permission. Keep your voice down. On narrow paths, be polite and offer the way to the person beside you. Dogs must be left at home, and babies, too, especially at private gardens, few of which can accommodate strollers. If it is raining, wear a poncho or bring a small umbrella that won't prune the trees as you pass under them, or need to be lowered into a flower bed, or lock spokes with another passing visitor.

If you meet the garden maker, offer praise. Don't criticize. Focus on what you see, not on what you have at home. I've had visitors come to my garden and spend the entire time talking about themselves and their own gardens. If you zero in on the owner's obvious pet plant, a flood of friendly and helpful information may follow.

It might be pressing the obvious to say that we shouldn't pinch cuttings or seeds or flowers or entire plants when we visit other gardens, except that it happens more often than we'd like to think. I've heard more than once, stories of people who pick plants and then ask the owner to identify the pinched piece. On the other hand, it doesn't hurt to ask. My way is to make an indirect appeal, in which I admire to acquire: "I love that plant, it's fantastic. Do you know a source for it?" Most gardeners have used a similar ploy often enough to take the hint.

JUNGLE FERVOR

Gardeners are sensualists at heart. We love intoxicating fragrances, voluptuous growth, and dazzling color. In a temperate climate, it is easy to accomplish this in spring and early summer, with bulbs and perennials and flowering shrubs. But carrying the garden through the heat of July and August so it still looks lively in the fall can be a challenge. After mildew strikes, flowers wilt, leaves crisp, and weeds are the only plants that seem to thrive, who hasn't been tempted to put away the trowel until the following spring brings a chance to start again?

John Beirne is never so tempted. As summer wanes and the scent of fall fills the air, his tiny northern New Jersey garden is heading for its explosive climax. That's because his plants have little regard for the seasons. The specimens that thrive in his narrow beds and numerous pots are tropical. They come from places that experience no shortening of daylight hours, no frigid temperatures. In New Jersey, the relentless sunlight, stifling heat, and high humidity of late summer just happen to provide the perfect conditions for nurturing sweet potato vines, hibiscus, bananas, cannas, castor beans, and elephant's ears. These energetic species, and many others, begin to take off when the dog days cause most other plants to fade, and they keep on going until they are finally cut down by the first killing frost.

John's garden is an annual experiment with new combinations of plants and colors. Nothing is too large or flamboyant for this young gardener, who fortunately failed to

learn all the proscriptions that garden taste-makers hammered into so many gardeners of an older generation. This lack of inhibition is most evident in front of the house, where he uses a series of tiny raised beds and pots staged on the little-used front steps to create what he calls "the psychedelic seventies island." On a street of two-story brick houses, each with mirror-image foundation plantings featuring all the usual suspects, this lush, vibrant miniature jungle stands out like a parrot in a robin's nest.

Although the house resembles others in the neighborhood, there is little familiar about John Beirne's exuberant plantings. The beds by the house have more in common with Chanticleer (page 161) than landscapes nearby. Exuberant arrangements of tropical plants explode in what might have been a conventional foundation planting with azaleas and somber yews clipped into tombstone shapes. Houseplants in pots decorate the planting dominated by a towering *Canna* 'Grande', OPPOSITE, while chartreuse sweet potato vine (*Ipomoea batatas* 'Margarita') spills onto the walk and overflows a planter box attached to the railing on the front door landing, ABOVE. PRECEDING PAGES: A detail of John Beirne's jungle.

"I wanted this to be as colorful as possible," he explains, accomplishing that goal with a scheme anchored by the startling chartreuse of the sweet potato vine (*Ipomoea batatas* 'Margarita'). The acid-green stems and leaves trail over the entrance path, then wind through a planting of pink caladium, red coleus, violet Persian shield, and ivory-streaked croton before finally embracing a towering *Canna* 'Grande'.

The bold foliage of cannas forms the leitmotif of the garden. Beirne flaunts *Canna* 'Pretoria', its almost fluorescent-green leaves pinstriped a creamy yellow, and the spectacular multicolored C. 'Durban'. Surrounded by all this color, the *Canna* flowers themselves take a few moments to register. 'Pretoria' displays deep-orange blossoms, and 'Phaison' bears luminescent papaya-toned blooms that seem to reflect a contrasting lavender hue.

But no one really looks for flowers in these beds. Foliage is the showstopper: the giant leaves (12 to 20 inches across) of elephant's ear (*Colocasia esculenta*), the black-veined imperial taro (C. 'Illustris'), the majestic red leaves of the castor bean plant (*Ricinus communis*), which towers five feet over the garage roof by the end of the summer. Even the *Hibiscus acetosella* 'Red Shield' blossoms are hard-pressed to compare with the plant's stunning maroon leaves, which resemble those of a Japanese maple. Like so many of John's tropicals, this one flourishes in overflowing containers, most of them hidden beneath trailing foliage by season's end.

Throughout the backyard John uses the plants that have made the biggest comeback ever seen in gardening: coleus, which have been liberated from the occupation of brightening sickrooms and ornamenting grandmothers' dish gardens. The new coleus don't

In the narrow bed against the west-facing, brick-red garage wall, OPPOSITE, giants flourish in a planting straight out of Star Trek. These plants, such as the broad arrowhead elephant ear (*Colocasia esculenta*), thrive in the hot, humid New Jersey suburban summers. RIGHT: Across from the garage, between the driveway and the back of the house, foliage plants grow in containers, such as feathery maroon hibiscus, several colorful varieties of coleus, and flowering *Lantana* species and hybrids.

even look like the old ones. Striking varieties, with big or little leaves bearing intricate patterns or solid colors, are being selected from seed lots and reproduced vegetatively, from cuttings, so they can be introduced and perpetuated. These colorful plants have evocative names such as 'Inky Fingers', 'India Frills', 'Purple Duckfoot', 'Ella Cinders', and 'Evil'. He grows all these and more, including a striking pumpkin-colored variety he selected from among mixed seedlings while working at nursery part time and which a friend named 'Beirned Orange'.

A lifelong gardener, John grew up collecting trees and other woody plants—the first of which, a rose-of-Sharon (*Hibiscus syriacus*), he transplanted from a neighbor's backyard when he was four. In grade school he forced winter branches to bloom for show-and-tell, and his favorite section of the supermarket was the plant aisle, where his mother often left him while she shopped. He begged his parents to bring him to nurseries, and he saved money from his paper route to buy his first mail-order plant, a tree wisteria from Kelly Brothers Nursery.

"The catalog showed this beautiful picture, so you can imagine how I felt when I opened the package and found a little stick," he recalls. "But I planted it, and it grew thirty feet." His love affair with trees continues, his latest crush being dogwoods sporting colorful

foliage. He has planted twelve, either on his property or on those of adjoining neighbors, including the rare *Cornus controversa* 'Variegata', with mostly white foliage carried on tiered branches that resemble a wedding cake.

Two events redirected John's horticultural passion from woody plants to herbaceous tropicals. In 1994 his biology class from Manhattan College, in the Bronx, took a trip to the Caribbean island of St. John. The goal was to study marine life, but it was the plants that captivated him. "The lushness, the colors," he says, practically swooning as he remembers the scene. "There was an extraordinary radi-

ance that I'd never witnessed before. Plants that struggled to survive in the corner of my mother's living room were a hundred feet tall and covered with flowers. I saw *Ficus* trees with trunks as big around as a Volkswagen Beetle. People there planted bougainvillea the way my neighbors use azaleas." John has returned to the Caribbean several times since. "Each time, by the end of the trip, I just know I'm going to move there," he says. "It doesn't help that when I come home it's usually thirty-five degrees out with freezing rain. But then spring comes, and I'm pretty much back here in New Jersey to stay."

Soon after that first Caribbean trip, John discovered a slightly less exotic spot, which turned out to be his second major horticultural influence. "I went for a walk in the neighborhood next to the college and saw a sign for the Wave Hill public garden," he recalls. "There I found plants I'd only seen in books, ones from remote, mountainous slopes of the world along with tropical plants in beds and containers, all growing happily outside." He wrote to Marco Polo Stufano, Wave Hill's director of horticulture, and got a job as a garden helper. "I couldn't believe I was actually going to work around the tropical plants I'd fallen in love with," he says. "And I knew if they could grow at Wave Hill, they could grow in my garden."

John's self-effacing demeanor belies his place as a great artistic risk taker. OPPOSITE: He had the courage to experiment with blue balls among the black-leafed taro and yellow-green philodendron near the variegated giant dogwood (*Cornus controversa* 'Variegata'). ABOVE RIGHT: Unlike the temporary painted objects and transient tropicals, the dogwood is hardy and will one day be the focal point of the garden. RIGHT: Not completely averse to subtlety, John planted a half-pot attached to the garage wall with trailing helichrysum and wandering Jew.

The job was only for one summer, but for the first time in his life he was surrounded by people who shared his passion, who taught him new gardening methods, new plants. He brought this newfound knowledge home, to the house he had grown up in and shared with his father. The property is tiny, less than a quarter of an acre, and the backyard, only 30 by 50 feet, doesn't leave much room to accommodate conflicting passions: the son's love of big, bold plants versus the father's love of lawn. John is quick to acknowledge his father's and late mother's encouragement, pointing out the largest tree in the yard, a double-flowering pink 'Kwanzan' cherry, planted with his father's help in 1984. "But the grass is my father's priority,"

he maintains, "no ifs, ands, or buts about it."

To protect his turf, the elder Beirne has for many years confined most of his son's gardening to foot-wide cement beds along the property's fence lines and the side of the garage. In front he allowed John to take over a small raised bed beneath the picture window, as well as the little-used front steps beside it, and tropicals in pots occupy a small concrete pad adjoining the back of the house. By the end of the summer these growing spaces, measurable in square feet, may as well be acres for all the color, texture, and interest they contain. But in spite of the garden's wild beauty, and the attention it has garnered—accolades from neighbors, newspaper and magazine articles, and its use as a setting for a

The arranged pots, beneath crape myrtle flowers behind the house, reveal John's attention to detail and passion for plants, BELOW. Pots of succulents flank a small round boulder. OPPOSITE: A view of the bed, opposite the garage and backed by his neighbor's, reveals how much is packed into this tiny space. The tree is a cherry John planted with his father; it is now in failing health, but the variegated dogwood has been planned as its successor.

catalog photo shoot—any plant that dares to grow onto the lawn becomes an endangered species.

"If my father gets to the lawn before I do, I have to go out and see what he's mowed over," John exclaims. "I've been fighting that for the past twenty-some years." The first plant his father ran over with the lawnmower was that very first rose-of-Sharon, which, in his naïve excitement, John had planted smack in the middle of the grass.

John has worked wonders within his father's restrictions, but like most young adults still living at home, he longs for a place of his own. "I would like to have a big enough garden to have rooms," he muses. "I want an English-style garden, with hollyhocks, larkspurs, delphiniums, lupines. But I also want a real funky tropical garden, and I want a succulent garden, and I want lots of containers. And I want enough space for everything to grow to its potential and not be on top of each other."

To some ears this longing may sound like an apology for all that he hasn't been able to accomplish. But to John, it is more a forecast of the future, an explanation of his plans and dreams. And there is one particular part of this vision about which he is not the least bit wishy-washy. Like many of us, John has what might be called the "backlash syndrome." If our gardens are minimalist, we long for cozy and informal. When that style begins to feel

cluttered and claustrophobic, we want clean and simple—again—until we find that sterile and cold. There may not be a solution, but by learning from mistakes and successes, the true dream garden will emerge. For now, John knows as much about what he doesn't want as what he does.

"One thing that I'm really adamant about is that I want no edges," he asserts. "I don't want to have any plantings near any fences or any walls. Every plant that I've ever grown in this garden is up against something: the walls of the garage, the side of the house, the fence. The other thing is: I want no lawn whatsoever. I never want to see lawn again."

Time will tell, but it certainly will be interesting to see what the future brings. Someday John will have his dream garden, and it may surprise visitors to see all the various styles and forms he contemplated years before—and to find him mowing the lawn.

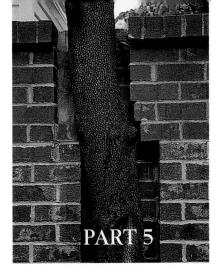

PART 5

COLLABORATIONS

I t is often said that art cannot be made in isolation, but every now and again, you hear about a recluse who for decades has created artworks that exhibit influences of classical or modern art. However, even a hermit gardener can never work alone. Gardening is always a collaboration between a person and at least one partner—nature. ꙥ Nature is never a silent partner, as any gardener knows, but it is usually working in our favor. It's good to remember that plants, like all

living things, are genetically programmed to survive. We know if we make a good bed, place plants in the ground and add water, they will grow. Baby plants do have a touch-and-grow period as their roots venture into new soil. But with just a little coddling, a well-sited plant will settle in and take off.

Besides being benign and beneficial, gardeners also know that nature can sometimes be furiously destructive. Since we can never be quite sure when such events will strike, many of us become fascinated by the weather forecasts, though we often desire different weather than that favored by the general population. We get angry when, deep into the third month without rain, the meteorologists forecast another glorious weekend. Glorious for whom? we wonder, standing under the accursedly cloudless sky, hose in hand. Maybe perfect garden weather only exists in our dreams. But while being unsure can be unsettling, it certainly is never dull. The vagaries of weather, which seem less logical as years go by, also make our gardening victories that much more triumphant.

While the weather can sometimes be capricious, there are other natural elements of our gardens over which we can exert some control. By rebuilding the soil we can make our beds either more retentive of moisture or quicker draining, and in that way more welcoming to a wider variety of plants. By removing invasive plants, we reduce competition for those we want to encourage to grow. Favoring natives helps nudge our land back toward the natural balance it used to maintain by itself, before human intervention. On every level, from campaigning to save a woodland to producing an earth-friendly patio—the pavers set in porous sand rather than solid concrete—logical steps can be taken.

An often-quoted gardening instruction advocates planting "the right plant in the right place." Providing you have good places for plants, and your soil wasn't stripped away during the construction of your house, this is excellent advice

Sometimes it is best to leave well enough alone. OPPOSITE: This magnificent specimen of the evergreen Sergeant's weeping hemlock (*Tsuga canadensis* 'Pendula'), located at Planting Fields Arboretum, Oyster Bay, New York, would be destroyed by pruning. Artist and machine make other shrubs successful. For example, Pearl Fryer clips hundreds of topiary, ABOVE, in his South Carolina landscape. RIGHT: Selecting the right plant for the right place may help avoid late spring damage from frost, which is what happened to the leaf and spathe tips of the Himalayan *Arisaema griffithii* that now resides in the Asian bed of the woodland in New Jersey.

to reduce maintenance. Circumstances and our desires for recreation may keep us from taking this narrow path, but the rule does have its applications. A shrub that grows naturally large is certainly best placed in a spot where it will have plenty of room—not in the foundation planting where, even with frequent haircuts, it will keep growing to cover the picture window.

The more familiar we are with the natural growth habit of our plants, the more successful we can be in getting them to accommodate our needs. If your need is to express yourself with topiary, this can be especially important, since certain plants take to this pruning regimen better than others. Beautybush (*Kolkwitzia amabilis*), which produces long arching canes from the ground, is not conducive to being pruned into a hedge, ball, or topiary shape. As with many shrubs that strive for an open vase shape, keeping a beautybush sheared would defeat the artistry and symmetry this plant carries in its genes, and likely will remove most of the flowers' buds as well. Gentle pruning—removing damaged wood, crossed branches, and clearing dead canes from the center of the shrub—will help the plant grow in a more orderly manner, prevent disease, and in the end, create something that looks beautiful.

On the other hand, think of a yew. Gracing the entrance of a pharmaceutical company near me is a wide circle of yews (*Taxus* spp.), across the road from a cornfield. Every winter, deer venture out of the nearby woods and browse the outside edges of this planting back to

bare wood. Every spring, the yews replace the loss with lush new growth, in time to be eaten again the next winter. These plants make great topiary subjects, as they can thrive through annual prunings for centuries.

Nature can also be called upon for assistance when it comes to figuring out how to grow a plant or create a specific

Climate, topography, elevation, sunlight, and shade—all of these factors affect plant success. Very often, it is the best policy to limit plant selection to those that will love the conditions your location provides. At times, however, niches can be found or constructed to provide wind protection, for instance, or stones to absorb and radiate heat in a cold place or a streamside to carry warm or cold air away. RIGHT: Hellebores have natural antifreeze in their cells so that even when covered in hoarfrost, the flowers and leaves perk up once the temperature warms. ABOVE: On a hillside in New England, Linc and Timmie Foster made a backyard that *was* a rock garden, capitalizing on soil and temperature. OPPOSITE: When in Arizona, plant as the Arizona desert does. Putting-green lawns would not even look nice in the pink light of evening.

garden bed. The most logical way to determine a plant's needs is to learn about the place where it originated. If a plant grows in the local woodlands, chances are that it will succeed in your patch of woods as well. If a species originated in the tropics and you live in Saint Louis, that could also be good news, since hot, humid summers might be just what the plant (if used as an annual) desires. But if I choose to grow a plant that does not come from my neighborhood, or isn't going to live year-round if plunked into any "right place" I may have, I need to try to mimic its original homeland. For example, if I want to grow plants that naturally live among rocks, it isn't enough to just pile up rocks, install a few plants, call that a rock garden, and hope for the best. The rocks need to be angled into the ground, so when it rains the water runs back toward the plants. If the plant comes from a spot where there is limestone, the soil should be alkaline. On the other hand,

if the plants were originally growing among granite rocks, the soil may have to be acidic.

We can also capitalize on the niches and microconditions that exist in any garden, no matter how small. For instance, if you want to grow a plant that originates in a higher elevation than your garden and doesn't like it hot, plant it in a spot where it gets sun up until noon but shade for the rest of the day. If there is a breeze in this location, all the better. If you have a plant that needs more hours of sunlight than your garden receives, try it in a spot where it might bask in the afternoon sunshine. For some plants, heat augments sunlight.

A plant that is marginally hardy for your climate might appreciate a place near a house wall or rocks that will absorb the heat by day and return it to the soil at night. However, growing a plant that blooms in late winter in such a warm spot may encourage the buds to open too early, leaving them vulnerable to being blasted on a freezing night. The same plant placed on the north side of a building, where the sunlight will not warm the buds until later in the season, may not suffer this damage.

HELPING HANDS

Asking for help in the garden shouldn't be hard, but it is for most people. Help is simply a tool, like many others we use all the time. You may need help to sort out your design, or a muscle facilitator to do heavy work, or someone with a plow to turn over the vegetable patch in the spring. If you're like me, you may be searching for the Holy Grail of helpers —someone who knows which plants are weeds, knows how to remove them, and will do so happily, tirelessly, weekly.

There are many reasons we need aid in the garden, some to do with the size of the task, others with our own strength or abilities or preferences. Consider what the payoffs will be for paying someone to do various tasks. Having a helper muscle out the stump of a long-dead tree can free you of a bothersome eyesore and open up new gardening space as well. If someone else mows the lawn, you'll have more time for tasks you prefer. I mow the lawn myself because I don't want to waste any experienced help I find on a chore I can so easily accomplish. Besides, it's hard to find teenagers to do this work at a price I can afford, and I have to admit that this chore is about the best exercise I get.

When I needed to find someone to help in my New Jersey garden, at first I was at a loss. I asked friends if they could refer me to their helpers, but they told me they were looking, too, and to let them know if I found anyone. At a local garden show I asked a man at the Master Gardeners' booth if he knew of a young person interested in horticulture who might like to learn and earn a little cash. He said he didn't, but asked if it had to be a young person. Of course not, I told him, and that's how Frank came to spend six Saturdays helping in the garden. Unfortunately for me, word got around about Frank's skill at recognizing and dispatching weeds. Soon gardeners better heeled than I were paying Frank what he was worth, and I was back to pulling the weeds myself. A short time later, Heidi volunteered to weed for free. She just wanted to learn, and we both weeded.

There are gardeners who love their gardens, but also know they could be better, and hire someone to help them realize that dream. Joyce Berger loved the plants she bought at local plant sales, and took good care of them. She felt that her menagerie needed a setting that befitted their most-precious status, and she also wanted an outdoor space in which to relax. Joyce, like many of us, had become "garden-blind"—the condition that sets in when we become so accustomed to something we can't see what needs fixing. She needed a fresh eye to help her visualize what her half-acre might become, and got it from Philadelphia-area landscape designer Tom Borkowski.

Tom immediately saw the solution: removing most of the driveway (a solution that many other gardeners might consider as well). There was no garage, but a wide lane of asphalt ran up one side of the house and wrapped around the back, ending at an unused basketball hoop. Tom left enough driveway in front to park three cars, dug out the rest and replaced it with a series of winding paths leading to a patio and planting beds in back. This area provided the perfect setting for Joyce's plants and many new additions. She loves the new garden —looking at it, being in it, and caring for it. The driveway, which she lived with for so many years, is now just a distant memory.

Sometimes we need a second pair of eyes or hands, or extra muscle or horticultural expertise, to accomplish certain things in the garden. We might want help for the tasks that do not require our skill, such as weeding or lawn mowing, or we might require professional help, OPPOSITE, as when horticulturist Louis Bauer excavated the roots of a young Japanese maple, covered the root ball with burlap, and prepared to move it to a new home. On other occasions, we may need a fresh perspective on our design, from a friend or a professional, to make the most of our plantings.

COMMUNITY

Many of us, looking to garden in a more natural way or to protect and preserve the undeveloped land that remains in our area, need to look beyond our own green spaces and collaborate with our neighbors. One piece of re-created habitat in a corner of one backyard can't provide enough food or shelter to attract any permanent animal residents. Likewise, pulling invasive weeds is great, but the good work ends at your property line. Encourage your neighbors to create and connect such restored areas into contiguous patches. Such neighborhood greenbelts and flyways can have a real impact (see page 117).

When fighting development, too, a large group of protesters certainly counts for more than a lone voice crying out in support of the wilderness. Politicians see these voices as votes, something I experienced firsthand a few years ago. The county engineers had revived a long-dormant plan to widen and straighten the road past my New Jersey property, which included the two one-lane bridges that lead onto and off of the island. The road was originally built in 1757, and winds through a nearly pristine watershed. The river is known to be home to at least two endangered species.

When the county workers began this project by cutting down a hundred-year-old black walnut along the road, I made sure the local newspaper was there to record it on the front page. On that day a dozen neighbors came to protest. A few weeks later, when the township board had the project on its agenda, 150 residents showed up for a meeting that usually only a handful of people attend. In the end, our protests were heard, and the plan was put on hold. New one-lane bridges—no wider or straighter than their predecessors—were built to replace the old ones. The engineers deemed them a "temporary" solution. But judging from how many local politicians were at the ribbon cutting, congratulating each other for this environmental victory, I think "temporary" will likely turn out to be permanent.

Collaborating with neighbors can not only help protect our own gardens, but is a way to extend our influence. I know one urban gardener who has convinced many of her neighbors to let her tend their front yards as well, which gives her more space in which to garden and benefits the entire block. Another friend lives in a densely settled suburb and wanted to screen out the views of his neighbors' houses, but didn't want the wall-like effect of a line of evergreens at the back of his garden. Instead, he got his neighbors to agree to plant a grove of unusual evergreen specimens on their various properties, each of them carefully sited to block out views in both directions. Creating community gardens in cities is one way to improve derelict vacant lots and bring neighbors together to make positive changes, as well as giving people with no other gardening opportunities a patch of earth to till.

Besides increasing our effectiveness, reach-

We learn everywhere we go, from nurseries, ABOVE; from gardens such as at Mohonk Mountain House, New Paltz, New York, OPPOSITE TOP, where we might learn about Victorian bedding schemes; and from estates open to the public, such as Old Westbury Gardens, OPPOSITE, where, with pencil in hand, we note plant combinations to reproduce at home.

ing out to the larger community of gardeners expands our knowledge. Visiting the public gardens in your area is a great way to find out what plants do well in your particular climate. We can glean information from picture books, from encyclopedias, and from mass media such as magazines, radio and TV, and the Internet. Dozens of good gardening Web sites, as well as chat rooms and news groups, can answer many basic questions and offer ways to visit virtual gardens and exchange information over the electronic backyard fence.

All state universities have cooperative extension offices, located in most U.S. counties, staffed with horticultural experts who can answer queries by phone and offer printed information by mail. These offices also run Master Gardener certification programs, in which serious amateurs take a series of courses in exchange for a commitment of volunteer time working in their communities.

A trip to the nursery is a learning experience as well as an opportunity to shop. Whether you buy or not, you will often see something new. You may go to a home-improvement center in search of inexpensive products or a cheap plant to rescue and learn another thing when you see plants bone-dry and near dead, or roses placed on dark shelves two months before they can go outside. It is forever surprising that these megastores don't even treat plants with the care given produce in the supermarket. I have to resist the temptation to rescue a

marked-down invalid, reminding myself that there is no such thing as a dead bargain.

Mail-order catalogs can be rich sources of information and dangerous to the pocketbook. Catalogs without color photos often have the most to offer in the way of information on unusual plants. The Heronswood Nursery catalog—256 pages at last count —written by nurseryman and plant explorer Daniel J. Hinkley (page 66), makes great reading on winter nights. There are too many other good catalogs to recommend here, but my 1996 book

Joining an organization, such as the North American **Rock Garden Society, or a plant group, such as the American Primrose Society, will put us in touch with others who share our interests and, sometimes, share their plants, such as alpines, BELOW, or *Primula sieboldii*, BELOW RIGHT. OPPOSITE: Two butterfly chairs patiently await their owners.**

The Collector's Garden profiles many of the gardens associated with mail-order plant specialists. Some of these places are open to the public at certain times of the year, and meeting the owners and staff presents a special chance to learn, firsthand, about the plants of your future.

We can also visit the gardens of neighbors and friends. After the second or third time you run into the same person at the nursery or in the garden book aisles at the store or library, you may have found someone with whom you can share your experiences. "I'll show you mine if you show me yours," the saying goes.

Soon after you begin gardening in earnest, you may discover a group of like-minded enthusiasts and a whole support system out there, waiting to help you. Some of these kindred spirits will belong to clubs and plant societies nearby, and others may live across the state line, the country, or even the world, reachable through the mail or the Internet.

You may be a member of a local chapter of one of the national garden clubs. You may join a society that specializes in your favorite plant or type of plant, such as the American (Hosta, or Rose, or Primrose, or Daylily, or Daffodil, or Iris, or . . .) Society, the Hardy Plant Society, or even the International Carnivorous Plant Society. Many groups focus on particular types of gardening, such as the North American Cottage Garden Society, North Ameri-

can Rock Garden Society, and the International Plant Propagators Society. Whatever your particular fascination, you can be sure there are others out there who share it. Many of these groups have local chapters, and most now have Web sites that make it easier than ever to connect with them.

PARTNERS

In horticultural relationships, as in other associations, there often has to be one person who is the gardener and one the flower. Two gardeners (read "strong-minded control freaks") end up butting heads, while with two flowers, little or nothing will get done. One couple I know have the perfect arrangement: she tends the flowers, he picks them.

Sharing a garden with a spouse or partner can be difficult at times. A two-person partnership is not a democracy—there are no other voters to break the tie or third branch of government to help decide if the tree should stay or go. Differences of opinion can lead to a lot of tension and there

isn't really a way out. One couple I know who have been gardening at the same time and place for over fifty years, suggest separate beds—separate garden beds, that is. I am not sure that such a drastic solution is necessary. But what if different areas of the garden are assigned so that one of the partners has the deciding vote? Both partners contribute opinions on the making and running of the garden bed, but one has the final say in a given area. Unfortunately, when I put this proposal up for consideration in my garden, the vote ended in a tie.

Rick Darke and Melinda Zoehrer (whose garden is profiled in this section) have a strategy of "tabling" ideas on which they disagree for later deliberation. The hope is that, after having time to ruminate on the topic, they will either develop a fresh approach, compromise, or agree to the original proposal. Geoffrey Kaiser and Bruce Grimes (see pages 131–143) recognize the taste and talent and particular interest of each other and defer in matters that favor one point of view or approach over another—or so it seems having survived nearly thirty years working on the same property.

LEGACY

The horticultural community is one of the few places in contemporary Western society where elders are revered for their wisdom. Part science, part intuition, knowledge of gardening is invariably cumulative, and while much of it can be read about in books, learning takes place in the garden, hands-on. Sharing is a hallmark of horticulture, and sharing this accumulated wisdom to help enrich the next generation may be the most important thing a gardener can do. And though it is important to pass on our love of plants and of the minuscule patches we actually garden, we need to do more. We need to show the next generation how one patch is connected to the neighboring patch and the next, and how ultimately our gardens are a part of the world.

My cousin Dan grew up on the Upper West Side of Manhattan, and like many parents, he wants to give his kids everything he believed he did not have. When funds allowed, Dan and his wife Fran moved to the suburbs. For two weeks each summer, Dan, Fran, son Caleb, and daughter Hannah go to the country, a beautiful lake community in central Pennsylvania. One year I was invited, and the first day I walked into the woods behind the house.

I didn't go very far. My goal is not to hike through the forest, but examine every inch of it. I stopped to stare at the first fungus I found, and a community of mosses thriving on a log. When I take my camera into the woods hours fly by, and I might not go more than fifty feet.

Dan and Caleb walked into the same woods later on that day and were gone for hours. When they returned, nine-year-old Caleb was hysterical. They had gotten lost, Dan reported. "And the worst thing is that Caleb will never go into the woods again."

Caleb had yet to learn the lessons which, through the millennia, have been passed from human to human. Gaining an understanding of the natural world is precious and a necessary part of growing up, but one that is more and more often neglected. I am sure that if a child is shown, at a young age, the frogs and bugs, birds, and even snakes outside and what these animals do to survive, they would find them more exciting than the latest video game.

I couldn't stand that Caleb's memory of nature would be a terrifying one. The next day, I begged him to walk into the woods with me, back into the very place he'd become lost in the day before. I said we would just go a few steps into the shade and see how we felt.

We walked about ten feet into the shadows, stopped and turned back to see the house.

Caleb and Dan became lost in a Pennsylvania hemlock **woods not unlike the climax forest that grows around the marble outcroppings at Bartholomew's Cobble in western Massachusetts, OPPOSITE. I went into the woods to examine the little mosses, ferns, and fungi that grow on the fallen trees and duff on the forest floor, and returned to show Caleb one of my discoveries: tiny sherbet-orange mushrooms, ABOVE.**

Then we walked further, and again, we looked back toward the house. I showed him the bright orange fungus I'd seen the day before and asked if he could find any other kinds. We looked at the twigs of saplings broken by deer, and the giant carcass of a fallen hemlock tree. We looked back to the house one more time, and then Caleb began to lead the way.

A camera can be the best way to document successes in the garden, as well as discover aspects of a design that can be improved. Most often we use our cameras to try to capture a moment in time, to remind ourselves of a very good thing so we can remember it and try to repeat it elsewhere. But we should also record our near-misses, such as plant combinations that didn't work and other things we don't want to repeat. Photographs can also help us project into the future, recording some of the things we hope to move the following autumn or spring. Of course, the camera can also document things we see in other gardens, public or private (but please ask for permission before taking any pictures).

Rick Darke has taken thousands of pictures of his garden over twelve years, providing him and his partner, Melinda Zoehrer, with a fantastic record of change. "Having photographs of a garden and its evolution is a wonderful thing," Melinda says. "It's incredible to look at how far we've come. It gives you a great sense of accomplishment." Rick points out that they can also be a reality check. "If you're a wishful thinker in the garden, you tend to delude yourself about what is or isn't there. The photo helps you say, 'No, that isn't right,' and redirect your thinking."

Rick knows that looking through a camera, by applying edges to the view, changes the way any garden appears. Even putting your hand in front of your eye like a telescope or framing the view with two hands will provide a new perspective. Problems that formerly melted into the view suddenly appear with crystal clarity.

If you have a point-and-shoot digital or film camera, take snapshots as often as possible. It might even be worthwhile to invest in an inexpensive camera to keep in the potting shed just for this purpose. If the camera has a date-and-time feature that marks the prints, turn it on for documentation. A photo album, with notes made beside or on the backs of the pictures, can be an excellent garden journal. An electronic journal can be made with a digital camera. Try out elaborate ideas for little cost by drawing on clear prepared acetate or tracing paper laid over color, or more useful, black-and-white photographic prints or ones made from the computer's printer. It's hard to imagine how much you will forget between the time you see something you want to alter and when you get to do it. You will also be surprised how much comes back to you when you see the physical reminder in the pictures.

In general, a slower film—ISO 100—will produce better color and less grain, and allow you to use the fill-in-flash feature on your point-and-shoot. Such a flash is useful when shooting in bright light, as it will brighten the shadows without bleaching out the true colors of flowers and foliage forms or altering the depth of the scene.

Try to take pictures in the evening, early morning, or on overcast days. At midday, when the sun is high in the sky, harsh contrast makes it hard to see results. In soft light, all of the colors (and less of the flaws and weeds perhaps) will stand out, but you will be able to see which combinations of plants are working well and those that are not. A tripod can also be helpful for the low-light situations, and, in general, to create the best photos showing the most area in focus.

You can use photographs to try out major undertakings. When Cheree Lucks built her elaborate walled garden in Columbus, Ohio, OPPOSITE, the view from the entrance had the neighbor's garage as its focal point. To show her how this "problem" could become an advantage, I took a photo of the site and sent it to Cheree with an overlay on which I had drawn a covered bench in front of the garage. I copied the handsome roof line of the building in the roof of the bench, which made it seem as if the garage was an outbuilding on the property. Instead of needing to hide the view, she would be able to quite easily incorporate it into the garden.

HEART TO HEART

Rick Darke and Melinda Zoehrer would be the first to admit that a grove of sassafras trees isn't the sexiest thing to put at the end of your driveway. The trees have no real flowers to speak of, and while their mitten-shaped leaves—fragrant when crushed—have wonderful autumn color, they are fairly common in the southeast corner of Pennsylvania. People driving by, who don't know that there is an unusual garden down the short driveway, might mistake the small grove for scrub the owner was too lazy to scythe.

Such an opinion would make Rick and Melinda laugh, considering the time it took them to settle on these trees as their uncommon solution to a common problem. Melinda is from California, where the courtyard—screened from the house and the road and from the neighbor—is a familiar garden element from Spanish colonial days. She wanted a way to extend the garden's front border to create privacy from the road. Rick, who grew up in a New Jersey suburb (where a democratic style dictates mirror-image lawns down to the curbside), never considered the front yard a space he would want to spend time in, so had never considered ways to make it more private.

Melinda proposed closing off the space after moving into the house where Rick had lived for three years. It was several years later that Rick proposed the sassafras grove as a solution. Small saplings were transplanted from a neighbor's property, and the fast-growing trees have satisfied both Melinda's need for enclosure and Rick's desire to

announce: "This garden is in southern Chester County, Pennsylvania, and it's all about regional motifs."

Regionality is the subject of this small garden, created on 1.5 acres of former farm field surrounding a simple stucco 1950s ranch house. But contrary to most gardens that pay homage to an indigenous look, this one is striking and beautiful, not merely a wood and meadow. In fact, the elements that make up

Although every season is beautiful in Rick Darke and Melinda Zoehrer's garden, autumn is arguably the best, when native grasses, tree leaves such as those of the dogwood, and herbaceous perennials turn color, PRE-CEDING PAGES. One such perennial is *Amsonia hubrectii,* a native with blue flowers in spring with wonderful feathery foliage that turns brilliant gold in the fall. ABOVE: Rick and Melinda like to point out how the beds have the shape and form of English herbaceous borders but have been planted with native species, OPPOSITE.

what we recognize as an ornamental garden are here but interpreted with many less-conventional species and cultivated varieties. The front border, for which the sassafras provided the finishing touch, is very much like an English flower border with waves of color tumbling over mounding plants and punctuated by spiky architectural specimens. But on closer inspection, the shapes and textures of foliage, in its herbaceous and woody specimens, are revealed even in high summer to be nearly bare of flowers. And in autumn, when this foliage catches fire and blazes in all shades of red, orange, yellow, steel-blue, and maroon, flowers would be redundant at best, if not completely lost in the show.

In back of the house, several large trees planted by the original owner, including an oak that towers over the house, provide a high canopy of shade beneath which many smaller trees and shrubs thrive. There are groves of other native trees: persimmons, silverbells, pawpaws, river birches. Along the sunny edge of shrub plantings, grasses grow in amazing variety. Rick worked for twenty years at nearby Longwood Gardens, where he was curator of plants. In that capacity, he was exposed to and became nearly obsessed by grasses. He grew his way through the trendy Asian *Miscanthus* and *Pennisetum* species and varieties and found that too many worthwhile North American species were being overlooked.

Many native grasses enhance the garden today. Rick hopes they will grow in popularity and eventually replace non-native—and in many cases, invasive—species. This goal has become something of a crusade in recent times. His 1999 book, *The Color Encyclopedia of Ornamental Grasses,* includes personal observation and advice as well as warnings about certain grasses—natural colonizers in their homeland—that are too aggressive to plant where they could escape into fields and meadows.

Rick and Melinda's property itself is adjacent to a farm field, and the view has been incorporated as a part of the garden. Beyond the field is a historic nineteenth-century barn,

Many of the plants selected for the garden have been chosen for what might seem unconventional reasons, such as the river birch (**Betula nigra** 'Heritage'), ABOVE, which is prized for its shaggy, exfoliating doe-skin bark. OPPOSITE: Native asters, such as purple **Aster cordifolius** and white **A. divaricatus,** produce a frothy foam along the path to the back door and across from the birches. OVERLEAF, LEFT: Grasses are Rick's passion and the subject of much of his writing. On the left is **Panicum virgatum** 'Northwind'. To the right of the bright red sumac (**Rhus glabra** 'Laciniata' is **Muhlenbergia lindheimeri.** RIGHT: A new selection of **Sorghastrum contortum** from coastal Delaware.

and beyond that a 3,500-acre forest preserve stretching up to the hilltop in the distance. Wide garden paths have been very carefully laid out and maintained to frame this view and others as well. The bucolic charm of the place is enhanced by a few pieces of garden art, among them a rusted tractor. With farms in the area rapidly succumbing to development, it serves as an evocative symbol of the local agricultural heritage.

The humble ranch house, rather than serving as a visual anchor for the garden, promotes an inside-out experience. Special scenes have been developed to be seen from inside, and the interior colors (such as the jade-green tiles in the dining porch) have been chosen to echo those of the garden outside. This idea

was most consciously planned when Rick and Melinda designed an addition. A bedroom with a high ceiling, it has large, curtainless windows that allow Rick and Melinda, while lying in bed, to see the treetops and sky and, at night, the stars and moon. Rick is hardly a Luddite; in fact, he is somewhat of a technophile, keeping up with the latest developments that relate to his many interests. But the couple has no televisions or air-conditioners, partly because they would block the sounds and fragrance of life outside.

"Sometimes there are so many birds in the garden, we wake up listening to all this singing," Rick says. "One night there was a mockingbird, singing at the top of his throat at about midnight. Wonderful things like that, and we've learned to just go with whatever is happening. The moon, too—the light of the last full moon—sometimes it drills a hole inside of your head and you wake up."

Although Rick and Melinda are enthusiastic champions of native plants, they are not purists. While at Longwood, Rick considered it important to try new plants at home, and among them were many exotic species. Melinda, who has a degree in ecology and works as a horticulturist at the Delaware Center for Horticulture, loves the variety of plants that could grow in the mild climate of her childhood. But both have come to love

Rick and Melinda do not always agree on everything, but they both feel that providing ways to get into and around the garden is crucial to good design. Some of their paths are wide, such as the one between the borders in front of the house; others are intimate, such as the grass path, OPPOSITE, on the side of the house that leads by the golden *Helianthus angustifolia* and to wilder, grassy places at the rear. In this shaggier, meadow-like place, Rick has made a sculpture, ABOVE, out of copper-clad sashes discarded after the renovation of a Longwood Gardens conservatory.

the feel of what Rick refers to as, in his often scholarly manner, "the eastern temperate deciduous forest."

Rick makes frequent expeditions into the nearby woods. He doesn't go to be soothed or to get away from the world. "I'm looking for provocation and inspiration," he says. "I'm excited about seeing patterns, smelling things, hearing sounds, and I find that it inspires whatever creative abilities I have. I might think about a melody and come back and play it on my piano. I might think about something I want to make, or a conversation I want to have, a photograph I want to take, something I want to draw. It's an emotional, sensual state."

"Living here has taught me a sense of connection to place, and I really like that sense of attachment, of belonging," says Melinda, whose father was a career Navy officer.

Not long ago, she and Rick were walking in the woods and they heard a moaning sound. Melinda mentioned that she'd heard the same noise the autumn before, and now a continuity of place has emerged for her. "This is the longest time in my life that I've lived in one place. I've been able to watch the landscape over the seasons and through the years."

The couple searched for the source of the noise. "We came to the woods, to listen and to look," said Rick. "And finally, we came upon two oak trees that were rubbing against each other in this wonderful way, they were making a ratcheting, groaning." They spent quite a while, looking, listening, remarking on the way the trees flirted with each other, touching and not touching. Someday, the trees may grow together into an embrace. "That's the kind of thing that fires our imagination," Rick says.

"What's exciting about the regional landscape is that it's evolving, there are so many rules that you can only guess at what's going to happen," he adds. "Even trying to understand any particular view: you can look at it as one big blob, or you can pick it apart into individual plants, or you can think about the way those trees have been shaped, by the light or lightning. You can intrigue yourself endlessly. So when I first got into actually gardening, I still wanted to make a landscape that makes me feel like I feel when I'm walking in woods and fields."

But how does one do that? At Longwood Gardens, Rick learned to create what he calls "contrived landscapes." He doesn't use the word in a pejorative sense—all gardens are contrived, after all. "But I don't get elated when I'm in those kinds of landscapes," he says. Longwood Gardens is famous for extravagant color gardens, enormous borders, and elaborate beds, but Rick and Melinda joke that when people come to see their garden, they might ask, "Where are the flowers?" Instead, Rick uses the garden as the basis of an intellectual narrative in which visitors can learn about things like the natural history of the area, or the aesthetic decisions that led to the framing of a view in a particular way. "I'm much more interested in those kinds of stories, as opposed to when you have people come to your garden and admire individual plants that may be beautiful but aren't native and may not even thrive in your area. It's a strange thing that people think it's wonderful when you keep something alive where, basically, it wants to die."

As time goes by, the garden is becoming more and more a showcase for the regional palette of plants. For Rick, who lectures and writes on the subject, the garden has also become an important testing ground for new plants and combinations, and the subject of thousands of photographs over the years, a number of which are included in his latest book, *The American Woodland Garden: Capturing the Spirit of the Deciduous Forest* (2002).

Because of this, Melinda finds she has to be careful about what she plants, and where she plants it. One year she grew *Salvia leucantha*, a voluptuous tender perennial she likes for its Mediterranean look. But this subtropical salvia blooms very late in the season, and she had planted it in the foreground of the long view of the adjacent field and woods. "Rick said he found it disturbing, and I

have to admit, it was a little discordant, it wasn't in sync with the rhythm of the landscape," she says. "Everything else around it was saying, 'I'm going deciduous, I'm going fall, I'm shutting down,' and it was just blooming and blooming. And that was the kitchen view, and you know how often you look at that view of your garden."

In planning and planting their garden, Melinda defers to Rick's need to keep certain vistas "purely native" for photographic purposes. "I will probably use that *Salvia* somewhere in the garden again," she says, "but not where it has a backdrop of deciduous woods and historic barn.

"One of the reasons we walk around the garden so much," Melinda says, "is to talk about what we might want here, or what we want to create there." It seems to have been successful, both for their garden and their relationship. "We like our garden, the feeling of being in it and looking at it from the house," she says. "We spend mornings on the tile porch, we look out, see it changing. It gives us a lot of pleasure. It gives us a lot of closeness, too, he and I. I don't think it's easy for couples to create things. A good relationship is a lot of work, it takes a lot of talking. And to create an extension of that, like a garden, is not easy. There will be some arguments—but in the end we can look at the garden, and say, 'We created this.'"

From the metal chaise, one of many pieces of steel furniture in the garden, the view is of the neighboring farm field, an increasingly rare sight in an area where farms are rapidly succumbing to suburban development. A nearly transparent sculpture of cedar poles constructed on the boundary between the garden and the field was originally meant to be a temporary ornament but has lasted for many more years than expected.

POINT OF VIEW

In the context of a garden, the word "view" can take on many dimensions. It can mean a single blossom, experienced close up as you lean in for a whiff of its aroma. It can be a long vista, looking past the garden to the ocean or hills or mountains beyond. It can be an outdoor scene framed by a window in the house, or a tunnel of greenery, with the light at its distant opening leading you down a darkened path.

There are two main considerations for capturing scenes in the garden: the object of the view, and the vantage point. The first of these is considered far more often than the second. More attention is usually paid to the placement of a bench in a lovely spot, as an ornament or something to see, rather than thinking of it as a place from which to see.

If you go around your property and isolate the special things to be seen, consider next the spot from which they might be viewed. Draw imaginary lines from a view to a vantage point and note the places that cross this line, along a path or even within an existing bed. These might be spots to develop reasons to take in the view. Perhaps the path should come to an end or a turn or have something placed at this point that will cause a visitor to hesitate. Plantings can attract the attention and carry the eye up and out towards the chosen view. A bench located within the bed, with a short path to reach it, will be both ornamental and a special spot to rest and take in the scene. You may have plenty of vantage points (for example, the view from the kitchen window) but far fewer things to

see (from that window, perhaps you look out at the side of the garage). Then the idea is to create the subject of the view: an ornament, or a planting that will be framed from this vantage point. To frame the diagonal view out to their neighbor's field, Rick Darke and Melinda Zoehrer created plantings on either side of it. To add some drama, they placed a see-through teepee of cedar posts to draw the eye out to the view (see preceding pages).

Exploring a garden becomes much more exciting when the whole is revealed piece by tantalizing piece, in little glimpses from the road or, as at my New Jersey property, from the porch, which hangs a full story above the ground level. The main garden is first revealed from this place, but it is a long view in which many of the details are blocked and obscured by large trees and shrubs in the foreground. The hidden details beckon, but when a visitor walks down the back steps of the porch to the garden even less of it can be seen, and then the enjoyable exploration begins.

I've used a number of tricks to make things seem larger or smaller, closer or farther away. In

In my New Jersey garden, in order to provide a high spot from **which to view the property, the top floor of the building's original unheated three-story addition was replaced by a deck. The "woodwork" of the new structure, ABOVE, is actually made of recycled plastic. The elaborate trellis, planned for a growing collection of vines, will never need repainting. OPPOSITE: The view from the deck is of the entire garden, including the round, cropped meadow and the woods beyond.**

1987, when I first laid out my Brooklyn garden (page 16), I arranged bluestone pavers along the path so that the largest ones were closest to the house, the most usual vantage point. The smaller stones were laid farther away from the house. This conceit exaggerated the perspective, making the space look longer than it actually is. The actual size of the open area of cropped meadow in my New Jersey garden looks immense from the vantage point of the new deck. When a person walks into the circle and to the far edge of lawn, the effect is a shock. The scale shifts when human scale is applied to the vista.

The curtain of columnar maples at the far side of the circular lawn draws the eye up, and forms a scrim in front of pine trees in the background. The plants are actually very close, but the layers of shrub border, maples, and background of pines make the border seem deeper than it is. The shrubs behind the gravel garden are progressively softer in color, from chartreuse to the silver-gray of pussy willow, creating a haze that softens the view into the distance. In several spots in the garden light-green foliage or variegated leaves have been used to brighten a spot and draw the eye (and the feet) ahead to explore a place that might otherwise have seemed like a dark dead end.

I am lucky to have real water, but there aren't many real views of it from within the garden. In an attempt to add "topography" to the mostly flat flood plain on which the garden sits, I took advantage of an opportunity when rebuilding the addition to the house. Instead of replacing the top floor of a former three-story structure, I made a roof deck with a railing. This gives me a high vantage point, one from which I often look at and photograph the garden below.

When planning for views, the place from which to see is as important as what is to be seen. Views can be borrowed and brought to the garden, whether they are on one's property or a neighbor's. But they also can be contrived, designed, and built by the gardener. Melinda Zoehrer planned an intimate view from one window of the house, RIGHT, one that cannot be seen either from outside in the garden or inside from any other room.

JUNIOR PARTNER

I've always dreamed of gardening. Not putting down my roots and laying brick paths with mortar, but feeling the soil, crafting plantings and nurturing plants. I remember shaping mud into pies, and scraping ravines through the soil with my toy bulldozer. I had a secret playhouse in the middle of a cluster of old rhododendrons, where I "gardened" on the dirt floor, planting sticks in mounds of scooped-up soil. I was the kid who rescued orphaned bunnies (with some success) and plants (with more success). One of the latter was a tulip poplar seedling that had sprouted in a gutter. I planted it next to our house in north central New Jersey, and though we moved from there long ago the tree still stands, now over thirty feet tall (and, I must admit, sited too close to the house).

I always drew pictures, sculpted, and painted. After college, I worked a few years in film, and then began doing botanical illustrations, which led me to writing about plants and gardens and photographing them. Along the way I have nurtured plants wherever I've lived: on windowsills in a college apartment; in tubs on a rooftop in SoHo, New York City; on a 21-by-50-foot plot behind a Brooklyn brownstone; and now on 2.5 acres in northern New Jersey.

I search for other outlets for my artistic expressions, but I always turn back to the garden, where I feel more confident about the results. In the garden, I know when a border is too narrow or the shape of the bed too blunt. I know if a combination of colors, textures, and form may work and can be proud

find myself thinking that gardening is just an escape, an intricate form of play—as if getting joy from any occupation somehow renders it illegitimate, turns it into something less than serious work. Gardening comes so naturally to me, and it gives me so much pleasure, and peace, that it hardly seems appropriate to say it is my calling. But there it is.

It is the gardening that calls me more than the garden, I think, and the various parts more than the whole: the rocks, soil, water, and especially the plants. To call me acquisitive is a gross understatement. I covet my neighbor's flora. I dream of certain must-have plants, wondering how and when I will ever get my hands on them. This is one reason I love having more space in New Jersey, and why someday I might move to an even larger garden, or one with different conditions that might give different plants a chance.

For me, the allure of gardening transcends the particular plants or even a particular place. It's about the process more than the product: taking part in the growth and change as the seasons go by and the years fly past. Each time we move on, we take with us the memories of success and failures, the experiences both magical and sad—along with as many of the plants as we can, of course.

My move to this New Jersey garden began about the time my Brooklyn garden hit its stride. The woody plants in the tiny backyard plot had grown several stories tall, and I, longing for more room, started looking for a larger piece of land outside New York City. In the fall of 1994, on my way to photograph a garden in Pennsylvania, I drove through the northwestern corner of New Jersey. This was the area I'd been dreaming of: close enough to my home/studio in Brooklyn, but with real mountains and rivers and lakes. I came back a

of it when it does, something I can't say about my other artistic endeavors. Lately I've come to wonder if, perhaps, I've been working in my medium all along—sculpting in partnership with nature, mud-pie maker grown up into garden maker. On the other hand, I still

A summertime view into the canal, OPPOSITE, from the arched stone bridge, ABOVE, is of a planting scheme in yellow and white, featuring varigated giant reed (*Arundo donax* var. *versicolor*), a gold-leafed ghost bramble (*Rubus cockburnianus* 'Aureus'), white-flowered feverfew (*Tanacetum parthenium*), and yellow-flowered variegated *Lysimachia punctata*. The giant reed is an aggressive spreader in warm climates, but works hard to produce a single shoot in New Jersey. The rambling ghost bramble never flowers there, and is cut to a single stem each spring to keep it in bounds. PRECEDING PAGES: The columnar sugar maples can be seen in autumn across the cropped meadow, their leaves a brilliant golden yellow. OVERLEAF: Lion gargoyles, cast from original architectural elements on a church in Rosyln, Scotland, guard the entrance to the sod-covered arched stone bridge that crosses the canal connecting the fast and slow branches of the river. The sculpture of Pan can be seen in its (probably) permanent place across from the end of the bridge.

few weeks later, armed with maps and real-estate brochures. The more sites I saw, the more my desires became clear. The house, I realized, was incidental. It was the land that interested me—and water, moving water. I didn't want a stock pond, or a hot tub, which was what turned out to be the "water feature" of one advertised property. In my paradise I imagined a babbling brook that, unlike my little Brooklyn pond, would have no pump or filter to clean.

After looking at more than thirty proper-

ties, I ventured out again on a raw December day, this time, dragging along two friends: Louis Bauer, then curator of the Flower Garden at Wave Hill, the public garden in the Bronx, New York, with whom I would make this garden; and Petie Buck, my childhood friend and a garden designer in New Hampshire. By the end of the day we were all cold, damp, and discouraged, and my companions groaned when I told them I needed to check out one more place. The ad said "water" and "motivated seller," and as we drove down a steep hill, past a grand eighteenth-century house, around an old red barn, across a one-lane bridge, and into a mist-filled hollow, Petie sat up like a shot.

"This is it!" she exclaimed.

Unfortunately, "it" was not the grand house and barn, but a squat green hovel plunked a few feet from the road. The property was dotted with dead trees, poison ivy, overgrown shrubs, and invasive weeds, but it had what I'd been looking for—an interesting, even eccentric parcel, with varied conditions—and lots of water. The house actually stood on the high part of a small island in a beautiful river, between the fast-flowing branch and a slower part that had been dammed for a long-gone mill. A narrow canal cut through the backyard, connecting one branch of the river with the other, and it was spanned by an arched stone footbridge. I was charmed by the stone walls built around the property, which served to contain the sandy soil reclaimed from the natural flood plain. Much later I learned that these walls also served to keep the river out, and that they worked only most of the time. But that first day, as we listened to the river rush along its rocky bed and over the falls of the dam, I began to think that Petie's initial response might just be right.

Even in the first exciting days after finding this property, I suspected the dangers of being on an island, surrounded by such an unpredictable force of nature. One tip-off was when my real estate agent told me that I would be required by law to purchase flood insurance. I conducted some informal research by talking to people who knew the

After the important trees had been mapped, an open circle was revealed, which, once cleared of brush, became the cropped meadow. Beds were made around its circumference, the first of which was the crescent-shaped border, ABOVE, developed along the north-west edge. The color scheme favors red and chartreuse foliage, seen in a blooming ninebark shrub trained into a standard, OPPOSITE, and flowers in shades from gold to brown, such as *Papaver orientalis* 'Patty's Plum' and one of many old iris.

site and heard various forecasts of flood probability, from "once in a decade" to "never." One longtime resident told me, "Not since 1938," which sounded reasonable to my hopeful ears: perhaps I had missed the last flood, and would not be around for the next one. I further rationalized that if bad floods had passed over this land, why didn't the mid-nineteenth-century foundation of the house show signs of damage or repair, and how had the old trees on the island survived? I deliberated, fretted, rationalized some more, but in the end the beauty of the place outweighed my fears.

It took five months to convince the allegedly "motivated sellers" to part with the house for just a few hundred dollars less than

the asking price. On May 1, 1995, the first moving van arrived, filled with hundreds of plants I'd been collecting since that mid-December day. Friends George Waffle and Jody Lathwell helped me plant them in a spot where Louis had created a nursery bed. In the open area on the far side of the canal we began clearing out the dead trees and shrubs, and over time we revealed a number of century-old specimens: a red Japanese maple and its middle-aged offspring; two mature *Chamaecyparis pisifera* (Japanese white cedar); a giant saucer magnolia; a blue spruce; and a few locals—hemlock and ash.

As I drew these trees on my master garden plan, I saw that they nearly made a circle, and Louis and I began to play with the idea of having them encompass a large open area. I saw, too, that the circular area would accommodate several things on my wish list: a perennial border along the northwestern edge; a shaded bed beneath the old magnolia next to the canal, which touches the lawn's eastern boundary; a shrub border at the south end of the circle. Louis put a stake in the ground in what we imagined to be the center of the circle, tied a line to it, and we walked around the circumference. When the circle's edge came too close to the canal or the drip line of a permanent tree, we moved the center stake accordingly or shortened the twine, and eventually we marked a circle ninety feet in diameter.

This area was to be a large lawn, which might seem surprising, since I have always been a champion of small lawns, or no lawn at all. But the open space, which provides much-welcome relief in this wooded and quite shady valley, is hardly a typical suburban putting green of plush velvet. In fact, I call my version of greensward a "cropped

meadow"—simply the grasses and non-grass plants (or forbs) that were already there, cut short (and never pampered with herbicides, fertilizer, or even extra water).

To make the perennial beds, we spread cardboard topped with chip mulch (made from the brush we had cleared) around the edge of the lawn. It took about six months for

The crescent border's color scheme proved challenging. Few plants come in shades like tan and toast. Peachy-yellow foxtail lilies, ABOVE, spike over a rare buff and green variegated *Polygonum* that commands respect for the reputation of its rampant kin, and so is planted in a 25-gallon tub sunk into the border. OPPOSITE: *Geum rivale* flowers in the right colors nod within the foliage of lady's mantle (*Alchemilla mollis*) and maroon *Lysimachia ciliata* 'Purpurea'.

it to kill the grass beneath it, and then the rotted cardboard and mulch were turned over with a spade and broken up with a fork to amend the sandy soil for planting.

Other areas of the property have been worked on in succeeding years, but the garden is still evolving, and like any garden I have ever made, it will never be finished. I will forever be tinkering, puttering, planting, changing, and moving this, adding or removing that. Seven columnar sugar maples, *Acer saccharum* 'Newton Sentry', were planted on an arc outside the circle of lawn, to reiterate its shape. A gravel garden in back of the house, home to many of the sun-loving, drought-tolerant plants I always dreamed of growing, is framed by a curving stone wall built by my neighbor Chris Hagler. Water-loving plants now grow along the canal on either side of the bridge. And I have begun to break into the circle of lawn with the first of what I imagine will be several plantings.

Having names for parts of the garden is like having words for the rooms in your house. You need to tell your partner where you'll be, or where something will go or could be planted. Between the "circle" and the "point" at the end of the island is an area of large trees growing close together, and that seemed a spot for the woodland garden. Under a large white pine and white ash, in a place that was used for a gravel dump, I scraped away the gravel, edged outlines of beds with logs, and filled the spaces with chopped bark, leaves, and compost. One large bed is now home to North American wood-land natives and across a wood-chip path, their Asian counterparts in an analogous bed.

A simple footbridge leads off island across the river's slow branch from the woodland garden. I've dubbed this near-acre mainland

which to grow interesting vines, where they could be watched and maintained. For ease of maintenance, the intricate trellis work for the vines and all the railings were made of white recycled plastic.

With the renovations, the house has become an attractive backdrop in views from the garden. Views from the house are important, as well, and this addition also has an accessible roof deck to give the garden the one thing a river valley property doesn't have: a high lookout point. I have taken scores of photographs of this broad view (as well as many more detailed shots) to record the changes and growth of the garden over time. I am amazed at how much parts of the view, at certain seasons, change from week to week, and how much, at other times, it remains nearly the same from year to year. It is nearly impossible to remember these changes, especially over the years, without the photographic evidence.

The rapid changes can be exhilarating (as in springtime) and the lack of change at other times makes me impatient for plants, such as newly planted trees, to grow and exhibit the reason for their choice and placement. But I love watching it. My ruling passion in the end, is just to look—and there are endless things to see in our garden, more than I can ever take in.

What astounds me is that I have had a hand in this, as a partner with Louis and with nature—but lest I grow too proud of my accomplishments, nature, the senior partner in this collaboration, has many ways of reminding me of my proper place.

The first year my worries about floods receded, as a summer-long drought caused trees to drop many of their leaves by August. But that fall I got a taste of what was to

part of the property "little new jersey." Over time, as we remove the aliens and beat back the invasive plants, we hope to create an all-indigenous "mitigation garden" (see page 112), a haven for the native plants that grew in this immediate vicinity before European settlers arrived.

Gradually, we upgraded the hovel of a house to an eyesore (one can live in an eyesore), with the focus of attention on the back, away from the road. I replaced the old porch when it became clear that safety was an issue. A three-story, unheated addition to the house served little purpose, and that came down, but a middle story was put back as an enclosed sunroom. This time, it was built without a basement so the nicest feature of the house, its stone foundation, would be visible. The addition was also to be a place on

Common wisdom dictates that a garden cannot be made with hundreds of only one of each plant, but that generally good advice would not do for this collector, and in 2000, the walled gravel garden was made for my obsessions. The wall, itself, RIGHT, is home to forty varieties of *Sempervivum*, BELOW. In the fast-draining crushed stone and clay soil, plants like border pinks, OPPOSITE, do very well, as can be seen with red *Dianthus* 'Waithmen's Beauty' and pink and white seedlings.

come, when the river rose as the remnants of a hurricane roared through. The canal filled up and overflowed across the garden, stripping the mulch off some newly made beds. We had two more floods within two weeks of each other in January 1996; a "thirty-year" flood in 1998; a "hundred-year" flood in 1999; and a flood the governor of New Jersey called the "millennial event" in 2000. (What could be next, I wondered.)

Then there was the freak tornado that came up the river on Mother's Day, 1996, and took down two of three red maples that grew atop the picturesque rock in the water off the point. And I'll never forget a wet, heavy snowfall of March 31, 1997, which draped itself beautifully over the early-spring garden. By the next day—April Fools'!—the snow had damaged or destroyed a quarter of our trees. On December 3, 2000, an ice storm encased the trees and heavy winds snapped the largest branch of the white pine in the woodland garden. The fifty-eight-year-old limb (we later counted the rings) came crashing down into the center of the oldest Japanese maple but, miraculously, caused little damage. The next day, Chris Hagler came over to help with the cleanup. As the chainsaw roared and we carried off pine logs, it began to rain, continuing through the night and into the next day. Waves from the fast branch of the river crashed against the stone

be doled out by the object of my adoration. Does nature test me as some people think God tests human beings? It doesn't seem to matter that I've tried to be good to nature over the years, promoting its cause in all my books, and with my checkbook and my vote whenever possible.

It's no surprise that a major player in many of these disasters—the river—is also the attraction and a source of the peace that I and many others find here. Houseguests are forever telling me that they slept like a log here. My mother says that when the trials of daily life become overwhelming she closes her eyes, imagines herself in this spot, and feels calm. Besides the color, the charming stone bridge, fragrant flowers and fresh air, the churn of the fast branch, the low roar of the water over the dam, and the babble of the canal create an ambient hum that soothes the soul and sets the restful pace.

Over time, I forget the results of the days that nature decides to throw a curve, and the changes wrought overnight are healed or absorbed into new plans for the garden. I might even be able to see them not as "disasters," but simply as big events in my gardening history, part of nature's cycle of renewal.

I have no choice but to deal with what nature doles out. It doesn't help, in the immediate aftermath, to think of the additional light that will now fall on the beds. I take no solace from a well-meaning friend's assurance of future "planting opportunities." But as I cart away the debris and prune the stubs so the plants can heal more quickly, I more quickly heal myself as well. Whether I like it or not, the garden is changed, but eventually I remember that change is what a garden is all about.

wall and flowed over and across the circle of lawn. The rain stopped but the river didn't crest until hours later, at 2:00 P.M. on December 5—the worst flood to date.

I recite this litany not to say that my lot is worse than any other gardener's. Things happen when we try to create sculpture in a living medium and the worst of them seem to

The woodland garden is divided into beds featuring plants indigenous to climates around the world that are similar to this site. OPPOSITE: A variety of local plants, such as *Phlox divaricata*, pink *Geranium maculatum*, and white *Tiarella* spp., bloom beneath *Halesia diptera* in eastern North America's bed. ABOVE: A pair of chance white *Arisaema* seedlings in the Asian bed in July. PRECEDING PAGES: The gravel garden in midsummer, LEFT, and late summer, RIGHT, of its second year.

MY GARDEN IN WINTER . . .

SPRING . . .

The first snow of December gives me and the garden a break, OPPOSITE, TOP. By March, the snow melts and the river swells, the fast branch of which can seen at right in its late winter peak, OPPOSITE, BELOW. One April, out of all the years I've lived on the island, the old *Magnolia* x *soulangiana*, TOP, bloomed without being nipped by the frost that normally turns its opening blossoms to mush that hangs on the tree until July. Later that year, ABOVE, the petals dropped as hoped.

Spring greens and new red leaves on Japanese maples introduce the most wonderful time in the garden, OPPOSITE, TOP, before the weeds and heat of summer arrive, OPPOSITE, BOTTOM, when roses bloom next to the sod-covered bridge over the canal. A killing frost can be expected in September, TOP, and all the leaves are gone by November first, ABOVE. OVERLEAF: On December 5, 2000, one of the more exciting events occurred, the property's eighth flood, reminding me that I am indeed the junior partner in this collaboration with nature.

SOURCES

I n the preceding pages I have stressed my version of the horticultural "Golden Rule." As gardeners, we should always strive to improve the health of the earth, leaving the places we live better off than we found them. This idea not only applies to our actions in the garden, but also to our treatment of the world outside our gardens' gates. As gardeners we have a special connection to the earth, which makes us the ideal advocates for the natural world. We need to pay attention to animal population imbalances, and to beware of exotic invaders whether they are insects, diseases or plant pests.

We need to speak out against environmental harm, doing whatever we can to limit sprawl, preserve open space, and protect the few natural areas we have left in this country.

For a listing of invasive plants by region, visit my website, www.kendruse.com. In addition, the larger conservation groups and native plant societies offer great information for gardeners. In Canada, the North American Native Plant Society is a great resource. In the United States, the New England Wild Flower Society is one of the top spots. That society's headquarters, the Garden in the Woods in Framingham, Massachusetts (www.newfs.org), is a wonderful place to visit (and buy plants). When purchasing wildflowers for your garden, be sure they are nursery propagated, not just nursery grown. Look for that claim if you see threatened species for sale at the big box stores—and don't buy them. The best way to get wildflowers is through one of the societies listed below and through sales at conservation groups and botanical gardens. If you see a potentially invasive plant for sale at a nursery or a botanical garden, inform the proprietor. When I see a plant such as purple loosestrife for sale at a nursery, I simply leave and do not purchase anything there. We have to have rules these days—that's the best way to give something back to the source of our enjoyment.

Center for Plant Conservation
Missouri Botanical Garden
P.O. Box 299
St. Louis, MO 63166-0299
314-577-9450
www.mobot.org/CPC

The Nature Conservancy
4245 North Fairfax Drive
Suite 100
Arlington, VA 22203-1606
703-841-5300
www.nature.org/

Plant Conservation Alliance
Bureau of Land Management
1849 C St., NW, LSB-204
Washington, DC 20240
202-452-0392
www.nps.gov/plants

Green Landscaping with Native Plants
77 W. Jackson Boulevard (G-17J)
Great Lakes National Program Office
Chicago, IL 60604
www.epa.gov/greenacres/

National Wildlife Federation
11100 Wildlife Center Drive
Reston, VA 20190-5362
800-822-9919
www.nwf.org

Society for Ecological Restoration
1955 W. Grant Road, #150
Tucson, AZ 85745
520-622-5485
www.ser.org

Wild Ones Natural Landscapers
P.O. Box 1274
Appleton, WI 54912-1274
877-394-9453
www.for-wild.org

Native Plant Societies

Among the many organizations active in local land-preservation movements, state and local native plant societies are the most active and most accessible for the individual gardener. These mostly volunteer groups work to protect the plants they love and their often-threatened habitats. Most groups have meetings, programs, publications, and websites to help you learn which plants are indigenous to your particular area, and which are the invasive thugs to watch out for.

Alabama
Alabama Wildflower Society
Caroline R. Dean
606 India Road
Opelika, AL 36801
334-745-2494
www.auburn.edu/~deancar/

Alaska
Alaska Native Plant Society
P.O. Box 141613
Anchorage, AK 99514
907-333-8212

Arizona
Arizona Native Plant Society
P.O. Box 41206
Sun Station
Tucson, AZ 85717
aznps.org/

Arkansas
Arkansas Native Plant Society
P.O. Box 250250
Little Rock, AR 72225
501-279-4705
www.anps.org/

California
California Botanical Society
Jepson Herbarium
University of California
Berkeley, CA 94720
www.calbotsoc.org/

California Native Plant Society
1722 J Street, Suite 17
Sacramento, CA 95814
916-447-2677
www.cnps.org

Southern California Botanists
Department of Biology
California State University
Fullerton, CA 92834
714-278-7034
www.socalbot.org

Theodore Payne Foundation
10459 Tuxford Street
Sun Valley, CA 91352-2126
818-768-1802
www.theodorepayne.org

Colorado
Colorado Native Plant Society
P.O. Box 200
Fort Collins, CO 80522-0200
carbon.cudenver.edu/~shill/
conps.html

Connecticut
Connecticut Botanical Society
Casper J. Ultee, President
55 Harvest Lane
Glastonbury, CT 06033
860-633-7557
www.vfr.com/cbs/

Connecticut Chapter
New England Wild Flower
Society
www.newfs.org/chapters.html

Delaware
Delaware Native Plant Society
P.O. Box 369
Dover, DE 19903
302-674-5187
www.delawarenativeplants.org/

District Of Columbia
Botanical Society of Washington
Botany Department, MRC 166
Smithsonian Institution
Washington, DC 20560-0166
www.fred.net/kathy/bsw.html

Florida
Florida Native Plant Society
P.O. Box 690278
Vero Beach, FL 32969-0278
772-462-0000
www.fnps.org

Georgia
Georgia Botanical Society
Teresa Ware, Treasurer
2 Idlewood Court NW
Rome, GA 30165-1210
706-232-3435
www.gabotsoc.org/

Georgia Native Plant Society
P.O. Box 422085
Atlanta, GA 30342-2085
770-343-6000
www.gnps.org

Hawaii
Native Hawaiian Plant Society
P.O. Box 5021
Kahului, HI 96733-5021
808-877-7717
www.philipt.com/nhps/

Idaho
Idaho Native Plant Society
P.O. Box 9451
Boise, ID 83707
www.idahonativeplants.org

Illinois
Illinois Native Plant Society
Forest Glen Preserve
20301 E. 900 North Road
Westville, IL 61883
www.inhs.uiuc.edu/inps/

Indiana
Indiana Native Plant and
Wildflower Society
Katrina Vollmer, Membership
Chairman
3134 Greenbriar Lane
Nashville, IN 47448-8279
812-988-0063
www.inpaws.org

Iowa
Iowa Native Plant Society
Diana Horton, Treasurer
720 Sandusky Drive
Iowa City, IA 52240
www.public.iastate.edu/~herbar-
ium/inps/inpshome.htm

Iowa Prairie Network
www.iowaprairienetwork.org

Kansas
Kansas Wildflower Society
c/o R.L. McGregor Herbarium
University of Kansas
2045 Constant Avenue
Lawrence, KS 66047-3729

Kentucky
Kentucky Native Plant Society
P.O. Box 1152
Berea, KY 40403
www.knps.org

Louisiana
Louisiana Native Plant Society
216 Caroline Dormon Road
Saline, LA 71070

Maine
Josselyn Botanical Society
Rick Speer, Corr. Secretary
566 N. Auburn Road
Auburn, ME 04210

Maine Chapter
New England Wild Flower
Society
www.newfs.org/chapters.html

Maryland
Maryland Native Plant Society
P.O. Box 4877
Silver Spring, MD 20914
mdflora.org/

Massachusetts
New England Botanical Club
Harvard University Herbaria
22 Divinity Avenue
Cambridge, MA 02138
617-308-3656 (Ray Angelo)
www.huh.harvard.edu/nebc

New England Wild Flower Society
180 Hemenway Road
Framingham, MA 01701-2699
508-877-7630
www.newfs.org

Cape Cod Chapter
New England Wild Flower Society
www.newfs.org/chapters.html

Michigan
Michigan Botanical Club
University of Michigan Herbarium
North University Building
1205 N. University
Ann Arbor, MI 48109
www.michbotclub.org

Wildflower Association of Michigan
Marilyn Case
15232 24 Mile Road
Albion, MI 49224-9562
www.wildflowersmich.org

Minnesota
Minnesota Native Plant Society
220 Bio. Sci. Center
University of Minnesota
1445 Gortner Ave.
St. Paul, MN 55108-1020
www.stolaf.edu/depts/biology/mnps/

Mississippi
Mississippi Native Plant Society
Ron Wieland
Mississippi Museum of Natural Science
111 N. Jefferson Street
Jackson, MS 39202
601-354-7303

Missouri
Missouri Native Plant Society
P.O. Box 20073
St. Louis, MO 63144-0073
web.missouri.edu/~umo_herb/monps/index.html

Montana
Montana Native Plant Society
P.O. Box 8783
Missoula MT 59807-8783

Nevada
Northern Nevada Native Plant Society
P.O. Box 8965
Reno, NV 89507-8965
www.state.nv.us/nvnhp/nnnps.htm

New Hampshire
New Hampshire Chapter
New England Wild Flower Society
www.newfs.org/chapters.html

New Jersey
The Native Plant Society of New Jersey
Office of Continuing Professional Education
Cook College
Rutgers University
102 Ryders Lane
New Brunswick, NJ 08901-8519
www.npsnj.org

New Mexico
Native Plant Society of New Mexico
P.O. Box 5917
Santa Fe, NM 87502
npsnm.unm.edu/

New York
Long Island Botanical Society
Eric Lamont, President
Biology Department
Riverhead High School
Riverhead, NY 11901
pbisotopes.ess.sunysb.edu/molins/libs/LIBS.html

New York Flora Association
New York State Museum
3132 CEC
Albany, NY 12230

Niagara Frontier Botanical Society
Buffalo Museum of Science
1020 Humboldt Parkway
Buffalo, NY 14211
www.acsu.buffalo.edu/~insrisg/botany/

The Finger Lakes Native Plant Society of Ithaca
Cornell Cooperative Extension
532 Cayuga Heights Road
Ithaca, NY 14850
607-257-4853

North Carolina
North Carolina Wildflower Preservation Society
North Carolina Botanical Garden
CB#3375, Totten Center
University of North Carolina
Chapel Hill, NC 27599-3375
www.ncwildflower.org

Western Carolina Botanical Club
Bonnie Arbuckle
P.O. Box 1049
Flat Rock, NC 28731
828-696-2077

Ohio
Central Ohio Native Plant Society
Jim Davidson, President
644 Teteridge Road
Columbus, OH 43214
614-451-3009

Cincinnati Wildflower Preservation Society
Victor G. Soukup
338 Compton Road
Wyoming (Cincinnati), OH 45215-4113
513-761-2568

Native Plant Society of
Northeastern Ohio
Jean Roche
640 Cherry Park Oval
Aurora, OH 44202
330-562-4053
community.cleveland.com/cc/
nativeplants

Ohio Native Plant Society
6 Louise Drive
Chagrin Falls, OH 44022

Oklahoma
Oklahoma Native Plant Society
c/o Tulsa Garden Center
2435 S. Peoria
Tulsa, OK 74114
www.usao.edu/~onps/

Oregon
Native Plant Society of Oregon
Jan Dobak, Membership Chair
2921 NE 25th Avenue
Portland, OR 97212-3460
www.npsoregon.org

Pennsylvania
Botanical Society of Western
Pennsylvania
Loree Speedy
5837 Nicholson Street
Pittsburgh, PA 15217
home.kiski.net/~speedy/b1.html

Delaware Valley Fern and
Wildflower Society
Dana Cartwright
263 Hillcrest Road
Wayne, PA 19087
610-687-0918

Muhlenberg Botanical Society
c/o The North Museum
P.O. Box 3003
Lancaster, PA 17604-3003

Pennsylvania Native Plant
Society
1001 East College Avenue
State College, PA 16801
www.pawildflower.org

Rhode Island
Rhode Island Wild Plant Society
P.O. Box 114
Peacedale, RI 02883-0114
401-783-5895
www.riwps.org

South Carolina
South Carolina Native Plant
Society
P.O. Box 759
Pickens, SC 29671
cufp.clemson.edu/scnative-
plants/

Southern Appalachian
Botanical Society
Charles N. Horn,
Secretary/Treasurer
Newberry College, Biology
Department
2100 College Street
Newberry, SC 29108
803-321-5257

Wildflower Alliance of
South Carolina
P.O. Box 12181
Columbia, SC 29211
803-799-6889

South Dakota
Great Plains Native Plant
Society
P.O. Box 461
Hot Springs, SD 57747-0461

Tennessee
American Association of
Field Botanists
P.O. Box 23542
Chattanooga, TN 37422

Tennesssee Native Plant Society
P.O. Box 159274
Nashville, TN 37215

Texas
El Paso Native Plant Society
Wynn Anderson,
Botanical Curator
Chihuahua Desert Gardens
University of Texas
El Paso, TX 79968
915-747-5565

Lady Bird Johnson Wildflower
Center
4801 La Crosse Avenue
Austin, TX 78739-1702
512-292-4200
www.wildflower.org

Native Plant Society of Texas
P.O. Box 891
Georgetown, TX 78627
512-868-8799
www.npsot.org

Utah
Utah Native Plant Society
P.O. Box 520041
Salt Lake City, UT 84152-0041
www.unps.org

Vermont
Vermont Botanical and
Bird Clubs
Deborah Benjamin, Secretary
959 Warren Road
Eden, VT 05652
802-635-7794

Vermont Chapter
New England Wild Flower
Society
www.newfs.org/vermont/
index.htm

Virginia
Virginia Native Plant Society
Blandy Experimental Farm
400 Blandy Farm Lane, Unit 2
Boyce, VA 22620
www.vnps.org

Washington
Washington Native Plant Society
7400 Sand Point Way NE
Seattle, WA 98115
206-527-3210 or 888-288-8022
www.wnps.org

West Virginia
West Virginia Native
Plant Society
P.O. Box 75403
Charleston, WV 25375-0403

Eastern Panhandle
Native Plant Society
P.O. Box 1268
Shepherdstown, WV 25443
www.epnps.org

Wisconsin
Botanical Club of Wisconsin
Wisconsin Academy of Arts,
Sciences, and Letters
1922 University Avenue
Madison, WI 53705
www.wisc.edu/botany/herbar-
ium/BCWindex.html

Wyoming
Wyoming Native Plant Society
1604 Grand Avenue
Laramie, WY 82070
www.rmh.uwyo.edu/wnps.html/

Canadian Wildflower
Societies

Native Plant Council
Box 52099
Garneau Postal Outlet
Edmonton, AB T6G 2T5
www.anpc.ab.ca/

The Wildflower Society of
Newfoundland and Labrador
c/o The MUN Botanical Garden
Memorial University of
Newfoundland
St. John's, NF, A1C 5S7
www.chem.mun.ca/~hclase/wf/
index.html

Nova Scotia Wild Flora Society
c/o Nova Scotia Museum of
Natural History
1747 Summer Street
Halifax, NS B3H 3A6

The Waterloo-Wellington
Wildflower Society
c/o Department of Botany
University of Guelph
Guelph, ON N1G 2W1
www.uoguelph.ca/~botcal/

Native Plant Society of
Saskatchewan
P. O. Box 21099
Saskatoon, SK S7H 5N9
306-668-3940
www.npss.sk.ca/

Botanical Gardens
and Arboreta with
Native Plant Displays

Arizona
The Arboretum at Flagstaff
4001 Woody Mountain Road
Flagstaff, AZ 86001-8775
928-774-1442
www.thearb.org

Arizona-Sonora Desert Museum
2021 N. Kinney Road
Tucson, AZ 85743-8918
520-883-1380
www.desertmuseum.org

Desert Botanical Garden
1201 North Galvin Parkway
Phoenix, AZ 85008
480-941-1225
www.dbg.org

California
Davis Arboretum
University of California
One Shields Avenue
Davis, CA 95616-8526
530-752-4880
arboretum.ucdavis.edu/

Quail Botanical Gardens
230 Quail Gardens Drive
Encinitas CA 92024
760-436-3036
www.qbgardens.com

Rancho Santa Ana
Botanic Garden
1500 North College Avenue
Claremont, CA 91711-3157
909-625-8767
www.rsabg.org

Santa Barbara Botanic Garden
1212 Mission Canyon Road
Santa Barbara, CA 93105
805-682-4726
www.sbbg.org

Strybing Arboretum and
Botanical Gardens
9th Avenue and Lincoln Way
San Francisco, CA 94122
415-661-1316
www.strybing.org

University of California
Botanical Garden
200 Centennial Drive #5045
Berkeley, CA 94720-5045
510-642-0849
www.mip.berkeley.edu/garden/

Colorado
Denver Botanic Gardens
909 York Street
Denver, CO 80206
720-865-3500
www.botanicgardens.org

Connecticut
The Connecticut College
Arboretum
5625 Connecticut College
270 Mohegan Avenue
New London, CT 06320
camel2.conncoll.edu/ccrec/
greennet/arbo/

Delaware
Mt. Cuba Center for the Study
of the Pedmont Flora
P.O. Box 3570
Greenville, DE 19807-0570
302-239-4244
(visitors by appointment)

District of Columbia
U.S. National Arboretum
3501 New York Avenue, NE
Washington, DC 20002-1958
202-245-2726
www.ars-grin.gov/na

Florida
Bok Tower Gardens
1151 Tower Boulevard
Lake Wales, FL 33853-3412
863-676-1408
www.boktower.org

Fairchild Tropical Garden
10901 Old Cutler Road
Coral Gables, FL 33156-4299
305-667-1651
www.ftg.org

Georgia
**State Botanical Garden of
Georgia**
University of Georgia
2450 S. Milledge Avenue
Athens, GA 30605
706-542-1244
www.uga.edu/~botgarden

Hawaii
Harold L. Lyon Arboretum
University of Hawaii
3860 Manoa Rd.
Honolulu, HI 96822
808-988-0456
www.hawaii.edu/lyonarbore-
tum/

**National Tropical
Botanical Garden**
3530 Papalina Road
Kalaheo, HI 96741
808-332-7324
www.ntbg.org

**Waimea Arboretum and
Botanical Gardens**
Waimea Arboretum Foundation
59-864 Kamehameha Highway
Haleiwa, HI 96712
808-638-8655
waimea.hi.net/

Illinois
Chicago Botanic Garden
1000 Lake Cook Road
Glencoe, IL 60022
847-835-5440
www.chicago-botanic.org

Morton Arboretum
4100 Illinois Rte. 53
Lisle, IL 60532-1293
630-968-0074
www.mortonarb.org

Massachusetts
Arnold Arboretum
Harvard University
125 Arborway
Jamaica Plain, MA 02130-3500
617-524-1718
www.arboretum.harvard.edu

**New England Wild Flower
Society**
Garden in the Woods
180 Hemenway Road
Framingham, MA 01701-2699
508-877-7630
www.newfs.org

Minnesota
**Minnesota Landscape
Arboretum**
University of Minnesota
3675 Arboretum Drive
P.O. Box 39
Chanhassen, MN 55317-0039
952-443-1400
www.arboretum.umn.edu

Mississipi
Crosby Arboretum
P.O. Box 1639
Picayune, MS 39466
601-799-2311
msstate.edu/dept/crec/
camain.html

Missouri
Missouri Botanical Garden
P.O. Box 299
St. Louis, MO 63166-0299
314-577-5100
www.mobot.org

Nebraska
Nebraska Statewide Arboretum
P.O. Box 830715
University of Nebraska
Lincoln, NE 68583-0715
402-472-2971
arboretum.unl.edu/

New Jersey
The Rutgers Gardens
Cook College
Rutgers University
112 Ryders Lane
New Brunswick, NJ 08901
732-932-8451
aesop.rutgers.edu/~rugardens/

New York
Brooklyn Botanic Garden
1000 Washington Avenue
Brooklyn, NY 11225-1099
718-623-7200
www.bbg.org

New York Botanical Garden
200th Street and Kazimiroff
Boulevard
Bronx, NY 01458-5126
718-817-8700
www.nybg.org

North Carolina
J. C. Raulston Arboretum
North Carolina State University
Horticultural Field Laboratory
4301 Beryl Road
Raleigh, NC 27695-7609
919-515-3132
www.ncsu.edu/jcraulstonarbore-
tum/

**North Carolina
Botanical Garden**
CB 3375, Totten Center
University of North Carolina
Chapel Hill, NC 27599-3375
919-962-0522
www.unc.edu/depts/ncbg

North Carolina Arboretum
100 Frederick Law Olmstead Way
Asheville, NC 28806-9315
828-665-2492
www.ncarboretum.org

Ohio
Holden Arboretum
9500 Sperry Road
Kirtland, OH 44094-5172
440-946-4400
www.holdenarb.org

Oregon

Berry Botanic Garden
11505 SW Summerville Avenue
Portland, OR 97219-8309
503-636-4112
www.berrybot.org

Pennsylvania

**Bowman's Hill Wildflower
Preserve**
P.O. Box 685
New Hope, PA 18938-0685
215-862-2924
www.bhwp.org

**Morris Arboretum of the
University of Pennsylvania**
100 Northwestern Avenue
Philadelphia, PA 19118
215-247-5777
www.upenn.edu/arboretum/

Texas

**Mercer Arboretum and
Botanic Gardens**
22306 Aldine-Westfield Road
Humble, TX 77338-1071
281-443-8731
www.cp4.hctx.net/mercer

San Antonio Botanical Gardens
555 Funston Place
San Antonio, TX 78209
210-207-3250
www.sabot.org

Utah

**Red Butte Garden and
Arboretum**
300 Wakara Way
Salt Lake City, UT 84108
801-581-4747
www.redbuttegarden.org

Virginia

Norfolk Botanical Garden
6700 Azalea Garden Road
Norfolk, Virginia 23518-5337
757-441-5830
www.virginiagarden.org

Washington

Bellevue Botanical Garden
12001 Main Street
Bellevue, WA 98005
425-452-2750
www.bellevuebotanical.org

Wisconsin

**University of Wisconsin
Arboretum**
1207 Seminole Highway
Madison, WI 53711-3726
608-263-7888
wiscinfo.doit.wisc.edu/arboretum/

Canada

**Memorial University
of Newfoundland
Botanical Garden**
306 Mt. Scio Road
St. John's, NF A1C 5S7
709-737-8590
www.mun.ca/botgarden

Montreal Botanical Garden
4101 Sherbrooke East
Montreal, QU H1X 2B2
514-872-1400
www.ville.montreal.qc.ca/
jardin/en

Royal Botanical Gardens
P.O. Box 399
Hamilton, ON L8N 3H8
905-527-1158
www.rbg.ca

**University of Alberta Devonian
Botanic Garden**
Edmonton, AB T6G 2E1
780-987-3054
www.discoveredmonton.com

**University of British Columbia
Botanical Garden**
6804 SW Marine Drive
Vancouver, BC V6T 1Z4
604-822-3928
www.hedgerows.com/
UBCBotGdn

VanDusen Botanical Garden
5251 Oak Street
Vancouver, BC V6M 4H1
604-257-8666
www.vandusengarden.org

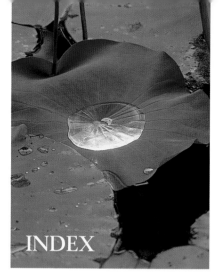

INDEX